Realizing Our Deepest Desires

Realizing Our Deepest Desires

Journeying into the Joy of God:
Reflections on St. Teresa of Avila's *The Interior Castle*

BERNIE OWENS, SJ

RESOURCE *Publications* · Eugene, Oregon

REALIZING OUR DEEPEST DESIRES
Journeying into the Joy of God: Reflections on St. Teresa of Avila's *The Interior Castle*

Resource Publications
An Imprint of Wipf and Stock Publishers
199 W. 8th Ave., Suite 3
Eugene, OR 97401

www.wipfandstock.com

PAPERBACK ISBN: 978-1-6667-3295-5
HARDCOVER ISBN: 978-1-6667-2718-0
EBOOK ISBN: 978-1-6667-2719-7

05/31/22

Sieger Köder, Der gute Hirte ©Sieger Köder-Stiftung Kunst und Bibel, Ellwangen www.verlagsgruppe-patmos.de/rights/abdrucke

To Mary, the mother of God,
And dear mother to me

also
To Aunt Mary and Uncle Ted Ryan
and
their three sons,
my cousins,
Tom, Dan, and Ted Jr.

In Memoriam
We Remember with Love and Sadness
Simone Pietro Abate
Our Smiling Angel
First-Born Son
And Only Child of
Giorgio and Maria Pia Abate
Died on November 3, 2007
In his 19th Year
Now in the Resurrection
With the Risen Christ
And the Communion of Saints

Contents

Acknowledgments

I MUST FIRST ACKNOWLEDGE the profound influence on me of my Jesuit companion and friend in Christ Fr. Michael J. Buckley, who in 1975 taught what for me was an unforgettable course at the Graduate Theological Union in Berkeley, California—St. John of the Cross's primary works: *The Ascent of Mount Carmel*, *The Dark Night*, and the *Living Flame of Love*. I learned so much in that course, especially regarding the genius, beauty, and spiritual depth of John's poetry and thought. But I also learned how to read and analyze a text and appreciate its logical structure from one paragraph or chapter to the next. Learning to appreciate the logical structure of John's writings greatly influenced my own teaching style.

I also began to appreciate the challenge and purity of the Carmelite way of thinking and journeying toward God. It has served as a wonderful complement to my Jesuit, Ignatian background with its in-this-world kind of spirituality. This attraction to things Carmelite which God worked in my life eventually took me to the writings of John's dearly beloved companion, St. Teresa of Avila. While her style and the organization of her subject matter are much different than that of St. John's, I found her writings to be equally engaging and often easier to grasp. It has been her final and greatest work, *The Interior Castle*, that has attracted me most, and I have eagerly chosen her vision of our soul/castle, with its seven dwelling places, as the overall structure of this book. It is God, then, through the wisdom and charm of Teresa, and through my own personal prayer, whom I happily credit with inspiring me to write this book. While Teresa wrote for cloistered women of her day, I am writing for Christians of all kinds and times, as well as for those of other religions and for anyone seriously searching for God.

Acknowledgments

My inspiration to write this book came also through the many students I enjoyed working with over the years when discussing the writings of Teresa: those in the seminars on Christian spiritual classics at Manresa Jesuit Retreat House in Bloomfield Hills, Michigan; then in courses on Teresa I led for African and Indian seminarians at Hekima College, the Jesuit seminary in Nairobi, Kenya; and finally, in a retreat for Carmelite seminarians and staff in Kenya.

I owe a great debt of gratitude first to Fr. Brian Paulson, provincial of the US Midwest Jesuit Province, for giving me a twelve-month writer's sabbatical in 2018–19 to finish this book, which I had begun in my last year at Mwangaza Jesuit Spirituality Centre in Nairobi. I am also grateful to the two Jesuit communities I have lived in while writing this book: first, the Pedro Arrupe Community in Nairobi, with the gracious encouragement of Frs. Terry Charlton and Leo Amani, its successive leaders/superiors, and also Berchmans House in Holland, Ohio, where I shared companionship with Frs. Brian Lehane and James Sand. I am also grateful to Fr. Miguel Garcia, director of ministries at Mwangaza, and Mr. Mike Savona and Mr. Chris Knight, president and chief operating officer, respectively, of St. John's Jesuit High School and Academy in Toledo, Ohio, for generously giving me time to finish this book.

I am also indebted to the following friends: Paul Siebold, Margaret Devereaux, Diane Neville, Mike Timm, Joe Olesnavage, and Kimberly Jumonville-Moore. They proofread the manuscript, brought their own special gifts/professional perspectives which wonderfully complemented one another, and made many valuable suggestions for improvement. Paul especially was a guardian of detail in watching for punctuation, and was of singular help in negotiating in German for permission to use the picture that appears on the front cover.

I owe special recognition and gratitude to four others who provided careful editing, making the text even better: Kristine Fauver, Sandy Harding, Rosemary Insley, and Sr. Anne Mary Molyet, SND.

I owe special recognition and thanks to Fr. Steven Payne, OCD, Carmelite scholar, author of numerous published materials, and to Sr. Marie Theresa Coombs, Hermit, PhD, co-author with Fr. Francis Kelly Nemeck, OMI of numerous outstanding works in developmental spirituality that use John of the Cross, Teresa of Avila, and Teilhard de Chardin as background. They were so helpful in giving me excellent suggestions for improvements, helpful corrections, and their endorsements. My thanks as well to: Fr. John

Welch, OCarm, a Carmelite scholar and author of *Spiritual Pilgrims: Carl Jung and Teresa of Avila*; Fr. Harvey Egan, SJ, professor emeritus at Boston College and author of works in Ignatian spirituality; and Mrs. Patricia Cooney-Hathaway, Professor of Christian Developmental Spirituality at Sacred Heart Seminary in Detroit, Michigan. They too gave me helpful comments, encouragement, and their greatly appreciated endorsements.

I also wish to thank some wonderful friends and helpful contacts in my obtaining permission to include toward the end of chapter 8 a poem I found quite fitting to the theme discussed there: Mary Counihan, Resa Pearson, Sr. Marcia Lunz, OSF, Sr. Diana De Bruin, OSF, and Mr. David P. Miros, Director of the Jesuit Archives and Research Center, who graciously granted me the permission.

I must also thank my friend of many years, Sr. Emma Bezaire, SNJM, for finding the source of the quote of her congregation's foundress, Blessed Marie Rose Durocher, cited in footnote 11 of chapter 13.

Then there are Christine Richmond and Gabe Gonzalez of St. John's Jesuit High School and Academy in Toledo, Ohio, and Kristine Fauver as well. I thank them so much for their generous assistance with computer-related challenges I experienced while writing this book and for helping me greatly with preparing the manuscript for the publisher.

So, too, many, many thanks to David Connelly, Ramy Eidi, Marie Molnar, and Bill Walborn, whose kindnesses, coming with God's amazing timing, helped me greatly to meet certain requirements related to the final preparation of the manuscript. Also, for the unconditional and steady gift of friendship from a true and faithful brother in the Spirit, Isaac Hanna.

I also acknowledge and express my profound thanks to a very good friend of mine who drew the six diagrams in the text. She has insisted that she remain anonymous. So be it!

Next, I owe a huge debt of gratitude to my Aunt Mary and Uncle Ted Ryan, as well as to their three sons, Tom, Dan, and Ted Jr., who for the fifty-four days following Christmas of 1958 prayed a rosary a day for a family vocation to the priesthood. Three weeks after they finished their prayer, God powerfully moved me while I was an engineering student at Marquette University, Milwaukee, to join the Jesuit order. I did not learn about this gesture of prayer till the following October, two months after I entered the Jesuit order. So many of the blessings of my life have followed from that singularly graced moment in my life. My eternal thanks to the Ryans!

Acknowledgments

Last of all, I acknowledge the unique place Mary, the mother of Jesus and Mother of God, has had in my life. With her prayers and love she has been present in so many of the critical moments of my life, and I believe she was very instrumental, through the rosary, in my coming to the Jesuits and persevering as a Jesuit and priest for 63 years. I was born on August 15, 1939, the feast day of her Assumption, took first vows as a Jesuit on that same feast day in 1961, was ordained a priest on June 10, 1972, the feast day of her Immaculate Heart that year, and then in 1991, on the feast day of her Immaculate Conception, December 8, I took my final vows when I was finally and fully received into the Jesuit order. None of these four days did I choose. They were all chosen, I believe, by God, through my parents or a Jesuit superior. To express my wonder and gratitude I took Mary's name to be my own when professing final vows in 1991. What providence to be placed so close to this exquisitely beautiful woman and friend in my life. As the days and years pass, I grow in appreciation of her humble gratitude to God and joy of heart, especially for how as a loving mother she shows such amazing love and care for me. Through the humble prayer of her rosary, I have experienced over the years how she leads us to know her Son more intimately, love him more dearly, and follow him more closely.

Introduction

THE DEEPER DESIRES OF our soul show who we really are and what we are willing to live, suffer, and die for. I begin addressing this theme of our desires by relating a recent TV news story that touched me greatly and reveals through our more profound desires the beautiful depths and divine possibilities in each of us.

THE STORY

Sophie Sanchez, a delightfully expressive ten-year-old, was desperately in need of a heart transplant. Typical of such patients, she had waited and prayed for nearly a year for good news. Her window of opportunity was narrowing, and she was suffering from periods of hopelessness over her situation. Then came the big moment when a new heart for her was available, but she had not yet been told about it when a local TV station was alerted and came to interview her. Sitting at the edge of her bed, Sophie was curious about this visit, anticipating her having to tell one more time about needing to wait for a new heart. With the TV station's cameras recording, a doctor came to break the wonderful news to Sophie. Her response was unforgettable and went national on the evening news.

With a look of astonishment, with eyes full of life and wonder, Sophie stood and exclaimed, "Mommy, Mommy! I am going to live! I am not going to die! They are going to give me a new heart and I am going to live, Mommy!" Watching her sob made for a very emotional moment, for me and I am sure for tens of thousands of television viewers. I was so moved by the sight of that young girl exuding the desire to live and of finally being relieved of the exhausting burden of fearing for her life. Her joy profoundly touched my own desire to live. What a powerful story for so many watching the news that evening! At the same time, it was a memorable instance of someone manifesting one of the deepest desires of our souls: the desire to live *forever*. Sophie's intensity also hinted at our soul's powerful attraction to goodness, truth, and beauty, and to what gives great meaning to our lives and promises us companionship. These strong attractions—above all our desire to live fully and forever—constitute the God-given drive propelling us forward to choose life, and eventually life with the Divine Source of our life, even to suffer greatly for it if necessary.

In the days following I found myself thinking often about this dramatic incident of Sophie learning that she was to receive a new heart, and with it there stirred inside me a correspondingly deep desire, like an echo of her own:

A PRAYER OF GREAT DESIRE

> Dearest God, I too am asking you for a new heart. As you promised through the prophet Ezekiel in 36:24–28 that you would pour clean water over your people Israel and remove their hearts of stone and give them hearts of flesh, so I ask the same for myself. Remake me, Abba Father, in the image and likeness of your Son, Jesus, so that, like Sophie, I may live a new and deeper life for you, and eventually give you all that I have and am. This is what I desire more than anything else.[1]

Not only did Sophie's great moment stir in me this prayer, but it also moved me, as has happened many times before, to wonder about the mysterious depths of the human soul and inspired me to probe the fascinating mystery of what prompts or evokes such powerful desires within us. How mysterious these expressions of our soul! How captivating the origin of these outpourings of our hearts and minds. They are strong manifestations of

---

1. God is beyond all names and gender distinctions. Yet we must speak about God and address God out of the poverty of our languages. While I am using traditional male language when speaking about God, imitating Jesus in so doing, I assure the reader of my sensitivity to this issue while avoiding gender-neutral ways for speaking about God. Such ways seem so impersonal and distant, contrary to the intimacy with God to which Jesus invites us. I respect those who prefer to address and speak about God with feminine names, like Amma, the loving name with which many people of Semitic and Arabic cultures address their mothers. Clearly, God is like the most tender of Ammas and Abbas who could ever be, and then far, far more.

a sacred juncture where God's Spirit and our own spirit are joined; they manifest how we are all beautiful images of the Divine and are made for eternal friendship with, and love for, each other. Deep, powerful desires come out of us, likened by Jesus to a powerful fountain of water gushing up in us (John 7:37–38). This divine water overflows and fills us with energy and strength to do what we often fear is impossible. We transcend what we were before while being led progressively by the Spirit of Jesus into a new depth of life.

It is this mystery of our depths and the unfolding of our more authentic desires that this book explores. I want to describe the process by which God draws out our good and better desires until we realize our deepest and best ones. To provide a strong framework for my presentation I am borrowing both the controling image and the basic structure St. Teresa of Avila (d. 1582) used in her classic book, *The Interior Castle*, to describe the human soul and its various stages of growth. She likens the soul to a castle made from crystal or a diamond.[2] The castle has seven concentric circles, each representing from the outer to the innermost circle a level of spiritual growth, with each level constituting a set of what she calls dwelling places, implying there are many rooms or variations in the experience of those in a particular stage. (She never names these rooms or differentiates one from another.) Once we step into our castle, we live in all seven stages to some degree, but predominantly in one of the seven at a given time. In the seventh and most interior of these dwelling places, we personally encounter, so beautifully, the risen Christ enthroned there. He welcomes us as the best of friends while we enjoy one another's loving presence forever.

In addition to insights from St. Teresa, I draw on teachings of St. John of the Cross, St. Ignatius of Loyola, and Scripture. John gives greater definition to the experience of the dark night than Teresa does. Ignatius gives us insight into disciplining our will and discernment as well as images of God that complement Teresa's images of God.

I am inviting you, the reader, to bring your own experience to the exchange between Teresa and myself, with John of the Cross and St. Ignatius of Loyola too. May you savor how God communicates himself with ever-increasing depth and richness to you and others. May this process illumine and inspire your own search for living more and more for God, eventually sharing forever in his boundless joy.

---

2. See Teresa of Avila, *The Interior Castle*, Volume II, Book I, Chapter 1, Section 1. Henceforth, *IC*, I, 1,1.

BRIEF OUTLINE OF THIS BOOK

In the first three chapters, I explore the process of God leading us to a basic interior order and peace. He coaxes us out of the moral chaos and spiritual blindness characteristic of life outside the castle and in the first two dwelling places. In the first two circles we experience some peace and a fragile moral order. By the third circle, or what Teresa calls the third set of dwelling places, we are empowered to live out, not perfectly but with a basic consistency, the Ten Commandments.

In chapters 4–7, I explore the challenges and obstacles we will wrestle with all our life if we are to grow beyond the third dwelling places. These chapters include: obstacles to faith, both personal and cultural; giving up control and learning how to receive both in prayer and in the relationships of daily life; and finally, facing our conscious and unconscious attachments and sinful habits/attitudes, the false gods we live for in place of the true God.

In chapters 8–11, I expound on dwelling places four through seven and offer my own reflections on these most important parts of Teresa's doctrine. There she explains the deepening purification and liberation God works in us when we are willing to leave behind what is not of God and allow God to usher us into the most intimate center, the seventh dwelling places.

In chapters 12–14, I focus on major implications in Teresa's text. Chapter 12 gives a summary of issues that come up regularly for those seeking a deeper spiritual life. Chapter 13, in keeping with Teresa's great emphasis on Jesus and his humanity, presents the Beloved Disciple in St. John's Gospel and how we can aspire to the deepest intimacy with God by becoming one of Jesus' Beloved Disciples. In chapter 14, I describe the kind of God Teresa experienced, along with how, in complementary ways, St. Ignatius of Loyola experienced and served God. In that closing chapter, I underscore what is so beautiful and attractive to our deepest self and how, because of this attraction, we are powerfully drawn into the depths of God. There, all creation, human and otherwise, enjoys communion with him in his boundless, abundant goodness and joy in giving life.

THE DEEPER DESIRES OF JESUS

In the context of reflecting on our deepest desires, we might profitably wonder about the depths of Jesus and speculate about the desires that welled up in him who was simultaneously fully human and fully divine. What came up in him, for instance, when, "a great while before day, he rose and went out to a lonely place, and there he prayed" (Mark 1:35)? Or on the last night of his life when, while agonizing in the garden, he poured himself out in words of fear and pain: "Abba Father, all things are possible to you; remove this cup from me; yet not what I will but what you will" (Mark 14:36)? Embracing our own life, and finding God especially in its challenges, can inspire us to ponder this intimate connection Jesus had with his Father and the Holy Spirit. It offers us a hint of what will characterize our own heavenly life—an unending outpouring of ourselves to Abba Father, to Jesus, and to all in communion with them. Our core desires, then, reflect the irrepressible movement toward God and our divine destiny.

> [This] dynamism of desire, [then,] means that every human being, [Jesus included], is a creature, that every one of [us] has been set in motion [by our Creator] toward [our] end, that the action of the Creator's Holy Spirit follows the bent of [our] being, orienting [us] along *the* natural path of desire. And so, we respond to the need [we] feel in the depths of [our] being, where each of us experiences the deepest movement of a created being.[3]

FROM TERESA AND MYSELF

I have written this book, then, after making a close study of St. Teresa of Avila's *The Interior Castle* and interfacing it with my own faith journey, my pastoral experiences, and my strong desires for God. Hopefully, it will serve as a map for many on their spiritual journey, while highlighting specific actions/disciplines we need to take in order to be more disposed to receive God's gifts. Perhaps of most immediate interest for the reader will be a description of the stage he or she is in now and knowledge of what is needed to cooperate with God in growing into the next stage. A thorough, careful reading through the entire book will offer knowledge and guidelines for spiritual directors and leaders of spiritual formation programs. May this book be a significant help and blessing for all who seek God with a sincere heart.

I have included at the end of each chapter a set of questions for discussion.

---

3. Conner and Fellows of the Woodstock Theological Center, *Dynamism of Desire*, 41 (emphasis original).

NARRATIVES AND DRAWINGS

To help the reader better appreciate what it is like for us to progress through these dwelling places, I am providing brief contemporary narratives—some from North American life, some from Africa—to illustrate various challenges and opportunities in these stages. Through these profiles I hope readers will gain greater clarity concerning Teresa's teachings and encouragement for their own lives with God.

I am also offering some diagrams to provide visual summaries of certain invisible realities related to our soul and culture. Like myself, some readers understand and retain better what is being presented if diagrams accompany words.

THE FRONT COVER

The picture on the front cover is a copy of a painting by Sieger Köder (d. 2015), a German Catholic priest. It depicts Jesus, the Good Shepherd, leading a celebration of the finding or rescue of the 100th sheep, now wrapped around his neck. This little creature had been lost but now is found, and this moment is cause for great joy both in heaven and on earth (Luke 15:3–7). It is my conviction that our personal stories of growing through the seven dwelling places are one long story of our being lost and found many times, saved by the amazing love and care of Christ, the Good Shepherd. The expression of emotion and brilliant colors in the picture suggests the joy in the Heart of God when any of us becomes free from our fears and false gods and trusts our deeper desires for a love that accepts us mercifully and welcomes us home.

Let us now consider Teresa's first phase of the spiritual journey: when people live outside their castle in terrible spiritual conditions and what they must do to begin to come home to God.

SECTION I

Early Stages

1

Desires Suppressed or Misdirected

THE OPENING CHAPTER OF St. John's Gospel depicts two soon-to-be disciples of Jesus noticing him. Jesus asks, "What do you seek?" (John 1:38). This simple yet profound question anticipates a progressive uncovering of their deeper desires. The disciples' response, "Master, where are you staying?" (John 1:39) is a beginner's attempt to search for God, for relationship, and for greater meaning in their lives. Their quest climaxes in a stunning discovery, revealed to us by Jesus on the last night of his life during his prayer to the Father in John 17. Jesus prays that we may know what he knows, realize in a communion with him and Abba Father the fulfillment of our deepest longings, and come to rest on his bosom.

On that glorious day we will have become fully who we were destined to be—fully human and, yes, fully divine,[1] transformed in Christ, shining forever with the brilliance of the Trinity. We will share in an eternal communion with cherished sisters and brothers from all times, lands, and cultures, and we will gladly intercede for those still completing their journeys on earth. Our hearts will finally be at rest in an unending banquet of joy and in the excited exchanges of our life stories and memories. Having taken on God's mind and heart, we will find our joy in the total gift of ourselves to God and to each other. This transformation will be a glorious revelation, far more than we could have ever asked for or imagined (Eph 3:20).

---

1. See Owens, *More than You Could Ever Imagine*, ch. 9.

While living with this glorious promise of Christ as described above, we will need to undergo conversion by facing our truth, usually awkward and humbling truths that at the same time are possibilities for new freedoms. As humans we yearn to connect, to relate, to belong. We desire to give and to receive, to be wanted and personally enriched through relationships, to discover the uniqueness of ourselves and encounter in our neighbor his or her unique goodness. As images of the Three-Person God, who is relational by nature, we are created to desire full relationship with God, with neighbor, and with our own self.

To gain a sense of what our deepest desires look like and who we are meant to become, I will start with a stark contrast. Let us imagine the situation of a person whose soul is in a disastrous state, with his deeper desires completely repressed. Teresa of Avila would describe this case as one who lives "outside his soul."[2] She emphasizes the tragedy of those who throw away their lives and completely ignore Christ, who is calling them from the center of what she images as their castle. By settling for a way of life that lacks all wisdom and is deadly, these individuals fail to discover their inner, God-given beauty and potential. Teresa depicts them as living out in the cold and dark, among rats, insects, and reptiles.[3]

AN EXAMPLE

A chilling example of someone slowly killing his soul, Art has chronically repressed the voice of God. Gerald May, in his *Will and Spirit*, pictures Art as a middle-aged salesman with "no time to waste with anything spiritual . . . We're just here by accident. There's no meaning whatsoever to it, so you just have to look out for yourself and make the best life you can. And there isn't anything afterwards either."[4] Art's joys, he says, are financial, sexual, and recreational successes. Joy "is getting what you want . . . getting satisfied."[5] He acknowledges nothing transcendent, nothing in art, music, nature, sex, or anything where he has felt "transported or awed or even nostalgic."[6] He does not express care for anything or anyone.

2. See *IC*, I, 1, 5.
3. See *IC*, I, 1, 5–6.
4. May, *Will and Spirit*, 191.
5. May, *Will and Spirit*, 191.
6. May, *Will and Spirit*, 192.

Art recollects a rather forbidding upbringing due to puritanical parenting. His parents forbade expression of any feelings: stoicism was how to be holy. Rebelling against his puritanical upbringing, Art:

> . . . denied their religion but accepted much of their repressiveness. This left him with even less than the meager narcissism they had. At least in their austerity they experienced pain and some degree of hope. But he was not even open to pain . . . pain was simply that temporary state of unrest that exists prior to gratification. He had no experience of despair . . . he said he did not even know what despair was . . .[7]

Yet Art does admit to frustration, but then quickly boasts that he is able to rise above such and move on to the next job, to the next woman, to the next fish to be caught. He is proud, he says, that he is honest and not like his parents, particularly in his allowing others to be how they want to be and not imposing himself on others. No pie in the sky for him either, he says: "I'm satisfied with what I get for myself right here."[8]

May recognizes that Art does have a philosophy of life and a value system; he has a god: the almighty buck, and he has a savior, namely himself. Meanwhile, he has closed his heart. There is anger and hatred inside him, most likely attributable to much emotional abandonment and hurt in his past. May says Art has "squelched his life-force. In the name of denying meaning, faith, and mystery he [has] denied joy and pain and any form of passion . . . [he has] denied, killed, even his own despair."[9]

It is this "life-force," as May calls it, that I will focus on in this book. I prefer to call it "the underground River of Divine Life," a phrase borrowed from David Hassel.[10] I will use these two expressions, as well as "Gracious Mystery"[11] interchangeably when referring to God welling up from our depths, initiating new life in us, and stirring our deeper desires.

Many who profess to be above religion, or are agnostic or atheistic, will admit that this life-force is spiritual in nature but refuse to recognize it as

---

7. May, *Will and Spirit*, 192.

8. May, *Will and Spirit*, 192.

9. May, *Will and Spirit*, 193.

10. See Hassel, *Radical Prayer*, 9–19.

11. Karl Rahner (d. 1984), a Jesuit and arguably the greatest Catholic theologian of the twentieth century, adopted this name for God while recognizing how God is beyond all names and ultimate mystery; at the same time Divine Mystery is the epitome of graciousness. Hence the name Gracious Mystery.

God. They love and enjoy creation but for various reasons will not acknowledge the Creator. However, as people begin to trust and allow themselves to
be led by this life-force, their soul opens to this Gracious Mystery and the
mystery of being loved and loving in return. They come alive! As Teresa of
Avila says, they finally enter their castle. Awareness of this transformative
power occurs later in an individual's spiritual development, after Gracious
Mystery is first acknowledged and welcomed. The challenge, then, once a
person does choose to trust, is "how close we can come to the fire, how
much of ourselves we can risk sacrificing in its flames."[12]

DESIRES, AUTHENTIC AND INAUTHENTIC

Desires are the stirrings of our soul, a movement toward what we perceive as
a good for our self and/or others. Usually, these stirrings are accompanied
by feelings reflecting our identity and values. The prophets of Israel, the author of The Song of Songs, Sts. John the Evangelist, Ignatius of Loyola, John
of the Cross, and Teresa of Avila, and other mystics "speak of befriending
our desires as vital to spiritual growth and discernment."[13] Our spirituality
is constituted by our various responses to the Holy Spirit moving in our
depths. Therefore, spirituality is intimately linked with our desires.

    There are various kinds of desires: some weak, some strong. Some are
superficial and fleeting, others come from the deeper levels of our soul;
some from the deepest part of us, our core. The diagram on the next page
gives us, as if we were looking into a deep water well, a visual sense of the
layers from which our desires emerge, as well as the levels of awareness in
us. Footnote fourteen explains in detail these four levels, which bears close
reading to appreciate what is distinctive of each level.[14]

12. May, *Will and Spirit*, 194.

13. Sheldrake, *Befriending Our Desires*, 10.

14 The first and most immediate level of our awareness, the sensuous-superficial, is
that of our senses through which we experience the world of people, animals, plants, and
the ecosystem of earth, sun, planets, and the cosmos. Here we feel pleasure and pain.
These experiences do not demand much attention and are accepted as part of the natural
flow of life. They do not last long in our consciousness.

The second level, the physical-vital, refers to our bodily functions and overall wellness
of body or lack thereof. These experiences demand greater attention than those of the first
level and affect the quality of our experience at the first level. They last longer and can be
more intense (e.g., a migraine headache or the good feeling following a vigorous workout).

The third level is designated the psychological-psychic level. Here we experience
deep joys and sorrows that can capture our attention for awhile, making us largely or

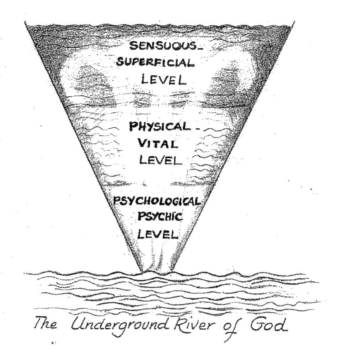

Diagram 1: The Underground River of Divine Life

The most important level is the last one, where the deepest part of us is immersed in the life-giving waters of God, the underground River of Divine Life moving there. From there we are continually being created, nurtured, and offered guidance.

We hear Jesus referencing this divine, dynamic reality when in John 7:37–38 he says, "If anyone thirst[s], let him come to me and drink. He who

---

completely unaware of what is happening in the first two levels (e.g., feeling anguish at seeing someone die or deep satisfaction in finishing a very demanding commitment, like an academic degree). Deep desires come from this level.

The fourth and last level is the level of spirit, both our own and God's. Called the underground River of Divine Life, this level represents the Mystery of God active in our depths welling up through the other three levels. It is where our greatest powers of awareness are found, immersed in the River, and the place from which our deepest, most authentic desires arise. Our awareness of the fourth level becomes habitual the more we spend time, with God's help, cultivating this awareness through meditation. Jesus is a prime example of such mindfulness. He found this level to be the wellspring from which he made his discernments and decisions regarding his ministry of teaching, preaching, and healing. See Mark 1:22, 27, and 35.

believes in me, as the scripture has said, 'Out of his heart shall flow rivers of living water.'" This river is uncreated. It has no beginning, has always been, and will be forever. It is the Source of all life, human and otherwise. In it we live and move and have our being (Acts 17:28). Deep desires prompt expression of our true and best self. The religious experience of humans from earliest times testifies powerfully to this Divine Mystery and Source of all life in our depths. This testimony is also evident in nature: in the earth and sky, in our sun and moon, in the stars and the entire cosmos. Relationship with this Mystery and desires for what is eternal have been expressed since the dawn of human life in the religions of the world in their stories, rituals, symbols, and art.

Some desires, however, can come from the first, second, or third levels of our soul, as indicated in the diagram, and can constellate as a false self by our becoming attached and identifying with them. Expressions of this false self can be: jealousy and envy leading to gossip and the desire for revenge; not wanting to get involved in something good and life-giving because it will "inconvenience me"; choosing to spend lots of time watching TV or on the internet to the neglect of commitments. These inauthentic desires appeal to our sensuality, materialistic values, and egocentric tendencies. It is possible to live habitually from these first levels of our soul where self-centered desires become our center.[15]

"The quality of a desire is determined by the object [of our desires]."[16] The quality of a desire is shown particularly in our intending to give our self to what is loving, kind, faithful, merciful, life-giving, and to what builds up relationships and shares with others. We seek what is good, true, and beautiful, and, at its best, we are open even to laying down our life for each other (John 15:12–13). "The more authentic our desires, the more they move us to glorify God. . . . [They] always lead us out of ourselves and into the human community. When desires to feed the hungry, to clothe the naked, and to use our gifts for the service of others become more compelling than private concerns, we . . . know . . . we have matured spiritually."[17] We are not only living in relationships *with* others, we are living *for* others.

The intensity of a desire, however, does not necessarily imply that the desire is more authentic—that is, coming from our union with the underground River of Divine Life—than one that is less intense. Certain intense

---

15. Summarized from Hassel, *Radical Prayer*, 7–19.

16. Kinerk, "Eliciting Great Desires," 3.

17. Kinerk, "Eliciting Great Desires," 4.

desires can come from one or more of the first three levels of our spirit, reflect a temptation to self-centered actions, and conflict with our true self. For example, deep resentments, intense anger, or strong sexual desire can be confused for what is deepest in us, only later to betray us and conflict with what we truly want and who we are. Vigilance and careful discernment are required to distinguish the authenticity and trustworthiness of our desires.

Usually, we live from a mix of authentic and inauthentic desires. John and James, the sons of Zebedee (Matt 20:20–28), are good examples. They chose to follow Jesus, an authentic desire. Yet, when encouraged by their mother, they petitioned Jesus for political success and power, an inauthentic desire. It would be their Pentecost experience and sharing in Jesus' postresurrection mission that would lead to the eventual purification of their self-serving, less authentic desires. In similar ways, we, like them, are purified when being faithful to our commitments, to our call to holiness.

A CULTURE GONE AWRY

Culture impacts our desires, for better or for worse. Let us focus now on cultural detractors typically found in today's Western culture but which are also alive in developing nations. The desire to live the self-centered consumerist lifestyle is the basis for the seven deadly sins: pride, greed or avarice, anger, envy, lust, gluttony, and sloth. They coincide with Teresa's description of the obstacles to entering our castle.

This way of living promotes a false gospel of happiness, success, and pleasure; it is where one's own wants are primary. A seductive ideology, it especially appeals to three types of individuals: 1) those who are given little or no religious formation or faith-focused upbringing, Christian or otherwise; 2) others who have turned away from a life of faith in God through long-term neglect, and 3) those who have disowned faith as irrelevant, boring, meaningless, or irretrievably flawed. This false gospel directs one's desires toward the good life and promises enticing rewards but not without exacting demands like excessive work hours and a pace of life where primary relationships and commitments tend to be neglected. Enticing to both Westerners and those in developing nations, this misdirected hope fosters a false sense of security in money and, especially in the West, a self-centered individualism, an attitude of entitlement, and little, if any, gratitude. It intends to satisfy our soul's need for God with indulgent shopping, entertainment, sports, and other pleasures of the senses. As *the* way for the liberated ones to live, this godless value system encourages *my* rights, *my* personal appearance, *my* body, doing *my* thing. It counsels us always to be in control and not impose my values on you so that you can pursue the way you want to live your life. The West has exported, far and wide, this false vision of a happy, fulfilling life.

Among the most egregious examples of this death-dealing lifestyle and its lucrative ways are: arms merchants who for billions and billions of dollars sell guns, bombs, and war machinery to governments and rebels in developing nations; those selling pornography, also for billions and billions of dollars; promoters of prostitution, abortion, and the selling of organs of aborted children; human-traffickers—the modern-day slave traders—and pederasts who molest defenseless children; and finally, those who sell addictive drugs that kill or ruin the lives of countless people. Then there are those who in international financial centers manipulate money markets and investments to serve their greed and lust for power. The disciples of this god of the economy displace millions of vulnerable people through joblessness, loss of financial security, homelessness, and mass migration.

Busyness is a major symptom of this dehumanizing false gospel. Desensitized people become less caring, less responsive to beauty and goodness, and no longer prioritize self-care, relaxation, or interest in the inner, spiritual world. Desensitized, dehumanized, and unresponsive, they slip into a superficial lifestyle. Disciples of this false gospel might claim they are spiritual but not religious. They can claim they talk to God, yet their actions betray no significant relationship with God. Their god is more like a Santa Claus filling the gaps, or is merely a projection of their own idealized self. Teresa of Avila, to emphasize how ill their souls are, says they have tragically chosen to live outside their castle in the dark and cold with the rats, insects, and vermin or worms.[18]

The people described above seek a god of some kind in their life. Their choice is some form of a superficial god-entity, a pathetic substitution for an authentic relationship and friendship with the real God. Their life-choice ignores the life-force or underground River of Divine Life, and eventually it catches up with them. Their vulnerability, human limitations and powerlessness, especially their mortality, are the gateways to the Source of Life, if only they will open themselves up to such graced opportunities. Paradoxically, these gateways are the door to finding the love we look for all the while. Until then, we are restless in soul and body.

18. See *IC*, I, 1, 5–6.

REVISITING ART: HOPE FOR HIM

Art's life of repression and excess will likely trigger an eventual collapse of his self-sufficiency and pride. Let us suppose he becomes terminally ill. No longer independent and self-sufficient, he finally accepts care offered by a compassionate nurse. If he does respond, the immense backlog of pain from his wounded past may manifest itself in a flood of anger and tears, and in his letting go of the need to control. He might even experience something of the deeper, core desires of his soul buried beneath his wounds. This vulnerability would be Art's best chance for meeting the loving God he never knew. He may even come to recognize himself as the prodigal son finally come home into the welcoming, merciful embrace of Abba Father. This is his doorway to hope and life eternal.

IN CONCLUSION

It is a great gift from God to admit to and give up the games we can play with God and finally surrender to divine love. Biblical history and every era demonstrate that some of us need to make numerous mistakes or experience ongoing powerlessness before we acknowledge this underground River of Divine Life flowing in our depths. We can keep delaying our response to the call of God, but someday, hopefully, we will finally trust and welcome the love and power of this Divine River. Christ, the Good Shepherd, the incarnation of this River of overflowing divine abundance, is so ready to lead us to the divine waters. There we can slake our deepest thirsts and be restored to our God-given goodness. He rejoices that, with our permission, he can now begin to lead us into the joys that God alone can provide.

Let us now look at what happens when one chooses to come in from the outside and enter his or her castle.

QUESTION FOR DISCUSSION AND FAITH-SHARING

- What details or aspects of Art's life, or of those referred to in general in this chapter, stand out the most for you? Have you met, or do you know or know about, people who appear to reflect this same spiritual state? Without getting into names, describe something of their state of soul and the fruit of their choices as it appears to you.

2

Entering Our Soul, Getting Started

EVENTUALLY A DAY COMES when living outside one's castle evokes feelings of emptiness and perhaps loneliness. This sense of void, of missing something deep inside, motivates the person to leave his or her desolate ways of living.

In the previous chapter we imagined Art coming into a new situation and awareness. In his infirmity and dependence, he would choose to trust life thanks to his finally letting someone care for him. The experience of compassionate care as a gift from God helps Art to let go of his pride and attitude of self-sufficiency, of not really caring for anyone except himself, and to finally enter his soul and meet God, at least in a beginning sense.

Entering one's soul and beginning the soul's journey to its center, into what Teresa of Avila calls the first two of seven dwelling places, presents some distinctive challenges. Often it involves a vacillation, a moving back and forth between one's past habits while struggling to acclimate to new ways of relating to God, self, and neighbor. I offer here a dramatic instance of this struggle. This example typifies the challenge of the burdened children of God who want to cut loose from their dehumanizing past and come home. This part of their journey is evocative of a scriptural parable: the one hundredth sheep (Luke 15:3–7), in its frequent stumbling, trying to discern the pathway home.

ENTERING THE FIRST DWELLING PLACES: AN EXAMPLE

Bonnie is a prostitute. She makes good money, but the better part of it ends up in the pocket of her pimp. He manages her work by allowing her enough for living expenses but little more. Doing tricks for an extensive clientele and using drugs has become a way of life for her the last two years. As time has passed, however, she has felt the growing desire to get out from under what has become a form of slavery.

One evening her emotional rollercoaster lifestyle comes to a head when one of her clients gets especially aggressive and demanding. He shouts at Bonnie, curses her for not performing as he wants and according to the stated fee. He throws a lamp at her, kicks her, and then, grabbing her by the neck, punches her in the eye. She falls backward to the floor, finds herself staring at a switchblade, and pleads for her life. He curses her again and runs into the night.

This is not the first time Bonnie has been beaten, but it is the first time her life has been threatened. Still lying on the floor, she thinks, *I hate this. I do not like myself!* Alone in the quiet and once her heart calms down, she touches her sore eye and mutters, "Enough! I have had it! No more, no more! Goodbye, pimp!"

And then it happens. An amazing peace comes over her, a feeling of being deeply loved by a Presence so total, stronger than all the tears she has shed over the years. Stunned and lying still for some time, Bonnie begins to weep, gently at first, but then gradually with greater and greater force. With her whole body she shakes, gasping and convulsing. *Might this be God?* she wonders. She feels her being held closely, tenderly, and reverently. Her mind tells her she does not deserve this, but she lets go and accepts what is happening. She feels wrapped in a love she has never known before.

It is a long time before Bonnie gets up and begins returning home. She has been captured by an amazing love. No one has ever cared for her like this, never! Yes, she feels terribly out of place, embarrassed, utterly unworthy, and yet so loved. She cannot go to sleep now, even though it is 2 AM. Slowly she walks one block after another, crying both out of joy and pain, sometimes stopping to sob against a tree. When she resumes walking, she is caught again by surprise, this time recalling a melody and the lyrics of a song she hummed years ago at a youth Bible camp: "I have called you from your mother's womb, you are precious in my eyes, and I love you." She now knows for sure that this love, this Presence, is divine. God has found her and is holding her to his heart. When she arrives back at her apartment, she falls into bed, totally exhausted, yet soothed by a sweet memory from her past and embraced with a new love.

As powerful as this moment is for Bonnie, her future is anything but smooth. Her dark moods and financial desperation make breaking away from prostitution very difficult. More than once she falls back into her former ways, only to become angry with herself and to find herself wanting to hide from her pimp. Each time he finds and beats her, though she fights back as best she can. Deep inside she knows she needs the help of addiction counselors, and especially of God, to escape once and for all this hell on earth, lest she die from this way of life or commit suicide. She prays intensely to be freed, to break forever from this intolerable way of living, enslaved as she is to an unspeakably oppressive man and to her own desperate longings to be loved. She begs to be given the strength to remain in the safety of the merciful, tender God with whom she has just recently reconnected.

Bonnie learns how to qualify for government aid. She checks herself into a drug rehab program and is now off the streets, beginning to love herself enough to cooperate with her counselors and learn how to pray. Despite occasional outbursts of anger and hatred toward her pimp and suffering moods of discouragement, she makes progress. She is choosing life and letting God open her up to the Scriptures, with their story of salvation—hers and everyone's.

As this case demonstrates, the people of this first stage or set of dwelling places are very fragile. They need much encouragement and help to continue their new way lest they regress to old patterns. Consumed by, and attached to, their own concerns, they are hardly ready to place God's will first. They hardly know God at this early stage. God is a last resort when their need is desperate. Their minds are too scattered, their hearts too broken, for their love to be more than feeble.

BRIEFER EXAMPLE

Driven by greed and pride, Jack is consumed by his work. But the recent drug-related death of his teenage daughter has shaken him to the core. His dream of becoming wealthy and widely recognized by his business associates now feels quite empty. He is filled with guilt about being a neglectful parent. He pours out his sorrow and grief to God and pleads for help. Facing this failure offers a new beginning for Jack; he promises God and himself that he will prioritize family over his work. He promises God that he will read the Bible and pray. He has found it helpful to talk with a pastor.

Yet as time goes by, Jack slips back into his old habits. He vacillates and is lured by the ambitious talk of his peers and seeks their adulation when he knows he should be home with family. He struggles with the tension between his authentic and inauthentic desires: the call of the underground River of Divine Life versus the siren call of worldly acclaim and riches.

GOD'S COMMITMENT TO US

God works with who we are and loves us in our present reality into new life. If Bonnie and Jack ponder some of the classic biblical passages expressing God's personal love for them, they will gain strength and healing. If they listen to God addressing them personally and if they remain aware of the more authentic desires that are now beginning to well up from their depths, they will progress from the first to the second dwelling places. As Teresa of Avila stresses, they must persevere in trying to remain connected to God, especially in prayer. Their prayer will be especially fruitful if, with experiences of God's unconditional love for them, they gain some insight into their self-centered habits and the ways they need conversion and healing.

Specifically, Bonnie will have to face her desperate need for love and especially the very unhealthy ways she has been trying to get it, betraying her deeper need. She needs to stand up for herself and live with God from the core of her soul. To get there she will have to be grounded in a stronger sense of her goodness buried under the present chaos of her life. Her challenge is not having to give up power, pride, and control—she has none of that now—but rather to accept and trust God reassuring her numerous times: "I have called you by name, you are mine . . . You are precious in my eyes, and honored, and I love you" (Isa 43:1, 4); and ". . . as the bridegroom rejoices over the bride, so shall your God rejoice over you" (Isa 62:5). Staying for days with these words while her spirit soaks in their tender love, Bonnie will become stronger in living with a new wholeness.

Jack's needs are basically similar, but his way for realizing them will be rather different than Bonnie's. Clearly, he will need to meet Jesus in a very personal way and see himself through the eyes of Jesus; i.e., seeing himself in the calls of Matthew (Matt 9:9–13) and Zacchaeus (Luke 19:1–10), both of them tax collectors living compromised lives yet invited by a loving Jesus into relationship with him; heeding Jesus' warning regarding attempts to

self-knowledge greatly impact the quality of our interpersonal relationships, our work, our ability to enjoy and be at peace with ourselves and others, and our capacity to pray and truly encounter God.

2. Second, the way for finding courage to face one's truth comes by way of looking intently at Jesus, recognizing our self in the Gospel stories, and/or through reading the life of a saint. Christ's goodness, or that of a saint, will highlight by contrast any of our self-centered ways; God's truth will expose our lack of integrity. The very human love of Jesus for us will win over our hearts to trust him and raise us up to new life.

The exciting part of this experience of being energized by this Divine River comes in moments when we immerse ourselves in Gospel narratives: finding how we are like Lazarus, bound and entombed by events past and/ or present (John 11:38–44); or like Mary Magdalene painfully searching for Jesus as she did on Easter morning (John 20:11–18); or finding a certain likeness to the Roman soldier, a nonbeliever, who was moved to faith in Jesus (Mark 15:39). Or, it might come in finding our self in the story of the woman caught in adultery (John 8:2–11), saved from execution by Jesus, who does not judge her because of her past but with touching care and sensitivity offers her a new future.

I have been privileged many times to witness this Divine Gracious Mystery saving people and inviting them into the joy that is God's. Like Moses meeting God in the flaming bush (Exod 3:2–6), whose fire does not go out, I remove my sandals, figuratively speaking, and bow face down in worship because I realize I am on holy ground. In these moments, I witness in myself and in the person I am guiding a wonderful feeling of being accepted, loved, and forgiven.

THE CHALLENGES OF THE SECOND DWELLING PLACES

Anytime a person commits to entering their castle, as Bonnie and Jack have done, and staying with the battle is a moment for great rejoicing, as pictured on the front cover. Yet Teresa stresses that the challenges in the second dwelling places are more intense than those of the first. It will take great courage, she says, not to regress, and a holy stubbornness to ask many times for the mercy of Jesus. People in this spiritual state will have to become aware, at least in a beginning sense, that there is Someone who loves them deeply, Someone whom they have deeply offended by their past. This often is their first sense of sin, of recognizing that sin is far more than just violating some moral code but rather is a failing to love the One who has deeply loved them. Teresa says they need to observe the commandments of God.[6] "In prayer, the life-giving Spirit of Jesus [will] illumine the dark corners of their heart. The images, thoughts and feelings that are part of the ever-present stream of consciousness that intrudes on our prayer . . . divulge content for conversion of heart."[7] Teresa says doing God's will, specifically changing behaviors, is "the whole aim of any person [in these second dwelling places]."[8]

EFFECTIVE PRACTICES

To reach these second dwelling places and not regress, beginners must become more serious about prayer. In the first dwelling places prayer is marked largely by formulaic prayer and urgent petitions, "God, help me" or "Jesus, I am in a lot of pain. Help me." In contrast, prayer in these second dwelling places is often referred to as discursive meditation, a reflecting upon Jesus and his encounters with the women and men in the Gospel stories. Prayer is now more reflective and increasingly nourishing to the soul.

Teresa cautions that the spirit that opposed Jesus and their growth in him manifests itself by stirring too much self-concern, for example, undue concern for their health or safety, or a clinging to whatever esteem they have had with the world, with friends and relatives.[9] Therefore, she stresses they must be attentive and make the most of the ways God is speaking to them: through the words of good people (spiritual guides especially), through sermons, good books, inspirations during prayer, or through illness and other setbacks.[10] Failing to follow through with these divine counsels is to risk falling back into a life of mediocrity, of capitulating and becoming a slave to the addictive-like demands of the senses; to a self-focused life

---

6. St. John of the Cross, in book 1 of *The Dark Night,* describes seven capital sins, which he stresses beginners in the spiritual journey must confront if they are to grow in the life of God. These sins are behaviors expressing pride, greed or avarice, envy, anger, lust, sloth, and gluttony. All of them are misuses of the life-giving energy God has given us. With divine help a person must wrestle with and make significant progress in overcoming these failings if he or she is to enter the third dwelling places and beyond.

7. Seelaus, *Distractions in Prayer,* 24.

8. *IC,* II, 1, 8.

9. See *IC,* II, 1, 3.

10. See *IC,* II, 1, 3.

characterized by fears and worries and being blind to or not caring about "other people's lives and the larger community and its concerns . . ."[11] They will never become autonomous, happy adults because they live according to the commonly referenced pleasure-pain principle (i.e., habitually choosing the easiest, most self-gratifying way at any given moment and avoiding whatever requires sacrifice and delayed satisfaction).

EARLY SIGNS OF TRANSFORMATION

The following metaphor sums up well this state of being:

> The second [dwelling places are] more like a railway station than a chamber of a castle . . . A railway station is for arrivals and departures. Everything is astir, charged with tensions of farewell, brave dashes to board the train which will take one far away from what one loves and clings to; second thoughts . . . delays . . . grief, fear, repugnance and also happy, mysterious anticipations . . . If we forego childish enjoyments we soon learn to appreciate the riches of maturer life.[12]

Those in these second dwelling places are making noticeable progress, showing a shift from being so self-focused. Priorities are changing. New freedoms are emerging despite the personal cost. Authentic desires are getting stronger, pointing them toward Christ, while they detach from inauthentic desires.

We turn now to the very interesting third dwelling places, including the intriguing question Teresa of Avila poses: Why do so many good people arrive at these third dwelling places but grow no further?

QUESTIONS FOR DISCUSSION AND FAITH-SHARING

- Have you encountered people in situations that are similar to those of Bonnie or Jack? Did life ever get any better for them or not? What seemed to be the core issue underneath their sinful behaviors that begged for conversion and healing? How did they experience grace/ the underground River? Did they waste God's gifts or grow with these helps of God to a happier, better life?

11. See Rolheiser, *Shattered Lantern*, 19.
12. Burrows, *Fire upon the Earth*, 26.

- Use Diagrams 1, 2a, and 2b to describe the spiritual condition of the Samaritan woman before she came to meet Jesus and then after their conversation (John 4:1–30).

3

The Third Dwelling Places:
Where Many Choose to Stay

ONE OF THE MAIN questions I have had for years from listening to many Christians open their souls to me is why, after a good and encouraging beginning in their life with God, so many do not grow further. They get to a certain point and stop journeying; they settle in. For me, like Teresa of Avila, this is distressing when I know something about the spiritual richness that could be theirs but which they are not taking advantage of.

THE CHALLENGE AHEAD

Teresa says there are many people who have won the battles described in the first two dwelling places of their soul and now find themselves happily in the third dwelling places.[1] They have successfully resisted the lure of turning back to their former attachments, thanks largely to their learning how to pray and drawing strength from knowing and loving Jesus. God has given them, she says, no small blessing in helping them get through the chaos and some of the self-centeredness of their past ways.[2] The challenge for them now is to remain faithful to God and to their new, reborn self by

1. *IC*, II, 1, 1.
2. *IC*, III, 1, 5.

going deeper with God. More specifically, this means they will have to give themselves to the demanding inner work of coming to know themselves better and endure a growing awareness of their sinful ways (i.e., behaviors and attitudes they were blind to before), and now appreciate better how displeasing these traits are to God. Teresa insists that if they are going to grow further in the life of God's Spirit they will have to renounce their pride and tendency of doing things their way and become accustomed to entrusting themselves to God and seeking his will much more so than before. Theirs will have to be, at least in a beginning sense, the bittersweet blessing of appreciating their own sinfulness and need for further conversion, of how greatly they need Jesus as a Savior and his Holy Spirit in order to enlighten and guide them. To say this differently: their coming to know what are traditionally called the seven capital sins or, better, the major spiritual disorders of the soul—pride, avarice, envy, anger, lust, sloth, and gluttony—with some or all of them alive in their life, will help them recognize certain areas of resistance to God that need healing. It will be challenging for them to look at this. Many avoid this inner examination, for various reasons I want to explore.

Those in these third dwelling places do take seriously their spiritual life, says Teresa. They often will adopt certain disciplines to curb tendencies to sin. They will choose to organize their time and possessions to maintain and promote inner spiritual growth. Many will choose a time for prayer, specifically to engage in discursive meditation, what Teresa calls active recollection, focusing on a Gospel passage, a psalm, or a story from the life of a saint, etc. While somewhat aware of their limits and inclinations to sin, they realize with much gratitude that they have made significant progress and their life has taken a very encouraging direction. But the enemy of growth, of what can be better, is the good. That is, the gift of God they receive now can become in time an idol. They can enshrine what they experience as progress and perceive these gifts that brought them into the third dwellings places as if they are the result of their efforts. This is a major temptation and common failing for those who have progressed this far into their castle. Teresa says the basic reason for their blindness is a lack of humility and self-knowledge: "With humility present, this stage is a most excellent one. If humility is lacking, we will remain here all our life—and with a thousand afflictions and miseries."[3]

---

3. *IC*, III, 2, 9.

TRAITS OF THOSE IN THE THIRD DWELLING PLACES

I want to dwell at some length on this obstacle because it can be critically influential in what direction we take with our entire life journey. Hopefully, this in-depth look will be quite illuminating for pastoral leaders and especially for those who truly want to grow in the Lord to appreciate well what are the traps and common pitfalls for those in this stage of the spiritual journey. If those in the third dwelling places cannot and/or will not acknowledge how true it is that their motives are often quite mixed and that they need deeper conversion, then they effectively halt any further growth in their life with God. For the rest of their lives their soul remains divided; they love God, but quite imperfectly because in some relationships and situations they love certain persons and things more than God. As I said above, the state of the soul of persons in these third dwelling places is a great improvement over the kind of life they lived before. Many would deem it their liberation from slavery. They experience a time of much greater peace, of psychological and spiritual stability more than they had in the first two dwelling places. But their temptation while in this new state can be experienced and voiced in something like the following: "My life is far better now than what it was before, thanks to my coming to Christ. I suppose this is as good as it will ever get for me, and it is pretty good. Who am I to aspire to something higher, to be very religious? I am not worthy of being a mystic or a saint. I will leave that to the spiritual elites. What I focus on is getting better at all the good I am doing now. I love it where I am presently and in my meeting many others of similar values and spiritual progress."

What is striking is that many of today's churchgoing Christians fit this profile. Fr. Tracy O'Sullivan, a long-time parish pastor, says in his paperback, *Pilgrimage to God: A Pastoral Theology of Contemplation for Pastors and Parishioners,* [that] "among church people the residence of choice is the third dwelling places. This choice includes both clergy and lay people."[4] He highlights from Teresa strengths and weaknesses in these good people, which we will now consider.

LOOKING CLOSER

First, they have a love for God that makes them try to avoid doing anything that would offend God, even in small matters. This love and reverence for

---

4. O'Sullivan, *Pilgrimage to God,* 47.

God will deepen and make them increasingly sensitive to anything the least bit sinful if they advance into the later dwelling places. They are eager to do penance and make time for prayer. In a way they are pleased with themselves that they manage to keep God as a key piece of what they call their busy schedule. They are usually good about caring for their neighbor and doing charitable works, while also being discreet in their words, their dress, and in managing their household. Teresa adds that she sees no good reason to think God would deny such people entrance into the seventh and final dwellings places, if they should so desire.[5] According to O'Sullivan, speaking from his experience, these people live "a serious and responsible moral life . . . [and are usually] committed to a [church] community of support."[6]

However, there is the other side to them. Their newly found freedom and progress of soul can tempt them to think they have arrived at an appreciable spiritual maturity; that now they are experienced and are quite knowledgeable about the spiritual journey, even ready to offer counsel to others. Sometimes this attitude is accompanied by rigid thinking, conservative or liberal, regarding church teachings and a suspicion of and resistance toward people who think differently than they do. With this mindset they are too satisfied, too out-of-touch with their own need for further conversion. They can also project their self-centered desires onto God, ignore certain teachings of Jesus, and thereby manipulate the Bible for their own purposes. Their images of God and Jesus are typical of those at an early stage of spiritual development (i.e., still rather influenced by self-interests: for example, personal priorities in earning and spending money, in vocational or career choices, in ways of judging the motives of family members, in seeking the esteem and praise of those in authority, in holding grudges, being jealous, competitive and envious, etc.). It can be said, then, that a little bit of knowledge or conversion can sometimes be a dangerous thing!

These characteristics of behavior and attitude are some of the typical obstacles that prevent people from changing, as a greater self-knowledge would suggest. Teresa says those who live in these dwelling places for many years and have avoided going deeper into knowing themselves can easily become upset and feel quite justified in complaining to God and others about some minor trial that has come their way. Considering themselves somewhat advanced in virtue, they think they deserve better treatment by

---

5. *IC*, III, 1, 5.
6. O'Sullivan, *Pilgrimage to God*, 43.

God.[7] The truth is they lack a spiritual depth that would enable them to suffer and grow in important ways from their trial. They do not know God very well because they do not yet know the Gospels and the humble Jesus very well, nor are they all that motivated to know him in his way of truth and humility. At this point of their journey their love for God and neighbor is like that of a well-intentioned but inexperienced adolescent. Their spiritual life is still marked by a lack of recognizing self-promoting habits they have carried over a lifetime, whether consciously or unconsciously, like perfectionist behaviors; needing to be liked; concerns about personal appearance (e.g., clothes, cars, and where they live); being defensive and needing to be right, especially in religion and politics; insisting on "my schedule," "my money," "my body," "my rights," "my choice."

EXAMPLES OF THOSE IN THE THIRD DWELLING PLACES

The biblical example Teresa cites to depict the kind of person in these third dwellings places is the rich young man in St. Mark's Gospel (10:17–22), described as one who has kept the commandments of God and upon whom Jesus looked with love. But when Jesus answers his inquiry about what he needs to do to become perfect, the man draws back. Selling his possessions to be free to follow Jesus more closely is too much for him. He loves his possessions and way of life more than he loves Jesus. His choice, then, is to compromise, to "look for some comfortable position somewhere between the Gospel and the 'world.'"[8] The young man might be afraid of an unknown future. Maybe parental expectations laid on him are too strong. Or the God he has experienced can be trusted just so far. Many possibilities. Some modern-day examples will help further our appreciation of this spiritual state.

Let us consider Jane, married and a mother of two small children. She was born into a religiously committed family and has remained a faithful churchgoer. From the beginning she comfortably adopted the style and habits of Christians in the third dwelling places. She has served as a catechist in her parish and as secretary for the board of her children's school and den mother for the Girl Scouts. She considers her donating blood twice a year and helping with voter registration to be the kind of duties that committed citizens should do. People experience her as forthright in expressing her views about these duties. At the same time, Jane is not shy about telling

7. *IC*, III, 2, 1 and 2.

8. Segundo Galilea, quoted in O'Sullivan, *Pilgrimage to God,* 47.

others what she is doing for the church, her family, and fellow citizens. She is critical of those who do not participate in local community services or go to church, and she feels justified in gossiping about those who, according to her, do not care enough about matters like this. Yet, she rarely finds time to visit her mother-in-law who is suffering from dementia, but instead prefers to pray for her at a rosary circle.

Then there is Fr. Newman, a church pastor, who has enjoyed being in charge of a parish for the last eleven years. He senses that the people mostly like him. Though not a great homilist or singer, he believes he leads an adequate liturgy and is convinced he has provided well for the parish during his tenure, spiritually and in material ways. He is known to be available to the troubled adult and needy child, giving spiritual counsel and even some immediate financial aid to some. He likes to promote events, particularly those that families enjoy and at the same time make money for the parish and its school. His wealthy friends and parish benefactors ensure he drives a nice car and sometimes take him to reputed restaurants, making him feel appreciated and rewarded for the kind of life he has chosen. He cannot imagine a better one. It is just about everything he ever wanted.

But the truth is that Fr. Newman's heart is marked with some mixed motives. He likes to control much of what goes on in the parish, school, and liturgies. The parish council and other committees are largely cosmetic. His clerical, controlling manner has fostered dependence and spiritual lethargy among his parishioners, nor has he encouraged any outreach to the needy in the nearby inner city. He loves it when a parishioner says he should have been a monsignor, if not a bishop. Not being named a monsignor prompts him sometimes to speak with resentment toward the powers that could have decided in his favor. They should have recognized, according to him, that he has done more than other pastors of his generation. Yet the truth be told, he has lived more out of the spirit of a careerist rather than as one having a vocation; as more of a church person rather than having a great love for Jesus and a strong desire to be his disciple and attract others to Jesus.

OTHER, BRIEFER EXAMPLES

There are those, often the extraverted personalities, who have to lead—in their workplace, church, club, local politics, etc.—or not be involved at all. If involved but not leading, they will often criticize those in charge and explain "the correct way it should be done!" They readily justify their judgmental ways: "I'm simply using the gifts God gave me" or "I'm just a committed Christian with high standards."

Then there are the introverted types, the shy ones who, from a false sense of humility, choose to be in the background. They do not volunteer but wait to be pulled in by others. They like to be alone with Jesus and enjoy saying their devotions. Their "Jesus and me" kind of piety is a common aberration for third-dwelling-place Christians needing instruction for a better understanding of Jesus and his way. They live often under a negative cloud, judging themselves unlovable and unworthy.

Also, there are those Christians who choose country over God. Patriotic and political values are sometimes more important and persuasive for them than Gospel values. Also, decisions about personal monetary investments are made without thought of justice concerns that Jesus calls us to include in our commitment to follow him. In short, their faith life is compartmentalized into the Holy (e.g., fervent about prayer devotions), and what they perceive to be outside the claims of the Holy (e.g., lacking moderation in their job/career and hurting their health and family).

Finally, there are those good people who have learned to avoid dealing with past hurts and their anger. They repress them all, sometimes in the name of doing what a good Christian should do. Others do the same with their sexual feelings, still others deny their excessive dependence on alcohol, and still others cannot face unresolved emotional blocks regarding certain authority figures.

LOOKING DEEPER INTO THEIR HEARTS

The fundamental option in life of those in these third dwelling places exposes them to a life with significant spiritual desolation because in many respects they are still the center of their life. Their "selfishness goes underground often taking on the guise of virtue. It hides behind good works and a multitude of good intentions,"[9] as observed in the above examples. In the moment of choosing, they will not entrust themselves in any ultimate sense to God. Rather, they prefer themselves and the security of what they know over God, even though they would probably not admit this nor even be that aware of their motive. Whatever the reason, they do not want to get too close to God or Jesus out of fear of being taken they know not where. With this attitude God can still guide them in a general way through the

9. O'Sullivan, *Pilgrimage to God*, 41.

commandments, but not to a much richer life of love and friendship with him found in the later dwelling places.

Furthermore, they often make their life and the lives of those close to them somewhat troubled ones. Burdened by their self-righteousness and ego-centered opinions, they judge themselves and certain others harshly. Again, like the rich young man, they tend to overvalue wealth and seek it for the sake of security, prestige, power, and privilege—what the empty gospel of prosperity and happiness promises. This orientation of heart significantly lessens, sometimes makes impossible, the chances of such Christians having relationships of any significant spiritual depth in marriage and family, in the priesthood, in the single life, and above all, with God. They think they know and are serving God, and in some ways they are, but in a fundamental, critical way they are not. This is truly sad.

O'Sullivan says, like Teresa, they have "to identify this self-deception with a new level of self-knowledge and growing humility . . . [There have to be] changes within . . . which basically make space for God to operate in an expanded manner."[10] Until then, they will assume that the blessings in these third dwelling places are good enough, perhaps even the most that Christians of their kind ever reach.

Before God leads them out of the fleshpots of their Egypt, their habits of self-promotion will remain a significant part of the way they think and interact in family and work. They might continue to gossip and criticize others, make excuses for their attitudes and actions, and hold on to their own small world where they feel secure and in control. They will admit, in a moment of false humility, that they are not perfect. Shrugging their shoulders, they will excuse themselves, saying, "But who, then, really is perfect? We are only human!" They will straddle life's alternatives and cling to the familiar and not allow themselves to get into a situation of committing unreservedly, of giving themselves irrevocably. Instead, they will hold back, protect the self they know, and choose not to venture into the unknown. They will avoid being vulnerable to deep love and its inherent risks to take them beyond their own limited life. This is the case in all their relationships, with God and with people. They will not enjoy deep friendships nor make good leaders unless they finally "cast out into the deep" (Luke 5:4) and quit trying to control God and their life.

10. O'Sullivan, *Pilgrimage to God*, 41.

LIVING YET DIVIDED WITHIN

In the spiritual walk, then, people of the third dwelling places love God *and* mammon: loving God to a degree, yet finding many of their interests and pleasures in the prevailing culture and its numerous empty distractions. They embrace a beginner's form of Christianity that is largely identified with religious traditions/devotions but does not look closely at the cross with any depth. Rarely do they see the link of faith with the needs for justice and care for the poor. Rarely, if ever, do they face the challenge of Jesus asking: "Who do you say I am? How much do I matter to you?" (Luke 9:20).

Instead, what these good beginners often adopt is an incomplete, sometimes even distorted version of Christ's church that is predictable in its sacramental rituals and soft or even totally lacking in its challenge to the values and politics of the surrounding secular culture. They can be Roman Catholic or Lutheran or Methodist or whatever, but not very Christian, not that knowledgeable about the Gospel. In time they can become jaded and bored with religion because they did not grow much beyond the beginnings of Christian spirituality. "Their hearts are open only to the limited horizon of their own immanence and interests, and as a consequence they neither learn from their sins nor are they genuinely open to forgiveness."[11] They stay busy with many things and tend to distract themselves with entertainment, sports, mindless TV programs, many hours on the internet, or other activities to satisfy their idle curiosity. They delay until the next life their having to look at whatever they did not face in themselves during this life. What Teresa insists on must be acknowledged if we are to journey into the later dwelling places. There, in the next life, the intense love of God will be unveiled, unfiltered, and will expose anything in us still self-centered, even the slightest manifestation of it. Until we are purged of such, we are not ready to meet God face to face, who is pure love, complete truth, and total self-gift.

Jesus met this same phenomena of settling for less in the spiritual journeys among the people of his own day. The story of the rich young man is not an exceptional case. In truth, this self-centeredness and resistance to Christ's invitation to a richer life in the Spirit has been there throughout the church's history. While concluding this chapter, let us look more deeply at how fundamental and critical is this call of Jesus; a call to the deeper

---

11. Pope Francis, quoted in O'Sullivan, *Pilgrimage to God*, 48.

meaning of our life and the opportunity there is for us to make the most of it and not let it fall through our hands.

THE HEART OF THE MATTER

In his preaching and teachings Jesus issued a clarion call to open to God in the present moment, in the now. He declared that the kingdom of God, God's powerful, loving presence and reign in and among us, is not just a future event but also a gift to be received especially in every present moment. God is coming, *in each present moment*, to our society and to every individual in it. He intervenes in our history, calls us to face our truth, to reform and be purified, and dare to love as he does. He saves us from spiritual death and recreates us, individually and as his people.

Jesus' stress on God ruling and saving in our everyday lives gives enormous, everlasting meaning to our own personal earthly history and the history of the world. The messianic expectations of the Jewish people have been realized. The long wait is over. God is *now*! He is not playing some game with us. This is not some dress rehearsal for a future performance. No, this is the great drama. Now is the day of salvation.

We need to catch the tone and power of this call in the opening of St. Mark's Gospel, where it is proclaimed with much drama that God's time has come. The message is: God has come very near to you. Pay attention, repent, change your attitude and your expectations, and believe in this event as Good News for you and everyone. This proclamation is not just a discussion about God's presence; no, it is telling us that this Divine Presence is already here, acting in our lives with power and everlasting meaning. It is now up to us how we will respond.

JESUS GOES TO NAZARETH

Such was the decision that faced the people from Jesus' hometown of Nazareth on the day he came to their synagogue. Invited to read and comment on the prophet Isaiah, he opened the scroll, read 61:1–3, and then stunned the assembly when he said that Isaiah's prophecy of God's anointed prophet liberating the blind, the lame, and the captives of Israel was now being fulfilled in their hearing, fulfilled *in him*. The future of God's covenantal promises was now! But the people who grew up with him and knew him as the carpenter's son were offended. They saw no significant change in their world. It was still cruel and unjust. They were still an occupied nation taxed heavily by a foreign, pagan army. How could he say God's rule had come? They had to wonder, "Is he deluded? Is he mocking us?"

Jesus insisted *much* had changed but that they were not open to recognizing it. He was speaking about the powers that cripple people's minds, souls, and bodies. He referred collectively to such forces as "demons."[12] God's power was driving out such powers, thereby reestablishing his rule among his people. The Nazarenes—and most of followers, including the apostles—were hoping for a prophet to lead the greatly desired overthrow of the Romans and establish a new, politically free kingdom. Jesus, however, was talking about something much deeper, something in the souls of people that would either free or enslave them, regardless of the political climate in which they found themselves.

JESUS COMES TO US TODAY

It is the same in today's world and particularly for those in the third dwelling places, not exclusively but still prominently so. "[A]pparently it goes against the human grain for God to become concrete in our lives. Then people's desires and favorite notions are in danger, and so are their ideas about time. It can't be *today*, because that would mean that our lives have to change *today* already. Therefore, God's salvation is better delayed into the future. There it can lie, hygienically and snugly packed, at rest, inconsequential."[13]

But God's coming is relentless and not just partial, not for the Nazarenes, not for us. Like them, we have a million and one excuses to delay God. Those of the third dwelling places, especially those who fit God into their schedules, feel like they have given so much already and are annoyed that he wants more, and wants it now. For Jesus there is an urgency about what he is proclaiming. He is declaring "the hidden treasure of the reign of God is already dug up, and the pearl of great value has already been acquired. The feast is ready to begin, and everything depends now only on whether those invited will come."[14] But the great challenge that makes so many hesitate or withdraw like the rich young man is Jesus' call to a

---

12. See Matt 8:16, 28–34; 10:1; 12:22–28; 17:14–21; Mark 1:21–27, 32–34; 5:1–20; 7:26, 29–30; 9:14–29; Luke 4:41; 9:1; 10:17–19; 11:14, 20.

13. Lohfink, *Jesus of Nazareth*, 32 (emphasis original).

14. Lohfink, *Jesus of Nazareth*, 35.

"surrender to the will of God, unto death,"[15] to personal sacrifice and a daily letting go and letting God. This is what Teresa emphasizes when she speaks about those in these third dwelling places, even more so in the four that follow. We will either hold back and try to save our lives (Mark 8:34–37; John 12:24–25), or we will allow God's Spirit to foster in us such a love for God that, like Jesus, we will increasingly entrust ourselves to God and his providential ways in our life. Our experiencing God as so good and loving will give us the courage to humbly admit the truth of our many imperfections and accept our powerlessness to pull ourselves out of this swamp, this unsavory part of our reality. Such an awesome grace and sweet blessing enables us to move into the fourth dwelling places.

More must be said about *how* to move into this new set of dwelling places. What can we do, then, to help this transition on which Teresa of Avila puts so much emphasis? Let us explore this now.

QUESTION FOR DISCUSSION AND FAITH-SHARING

- What does the challenge of Jesus to his hometown folks challenge in you and in your life?

---

15. Lohfink, *Jesus of Nazareth*, 38.

SECTION II

Challenges and Obstacles in
the Latter Dwelling Places

4

Obstacles to Faith

IN THE PREVIOUS CHAPTER, the words spoken by Jesus in the synagogue of his hometown of Nazareth evoked a powerful reaction. He bluntly told his people they were closed to God, that their lack of faith left little room for God to do anything significant in them. This proclamation nearly got him killed (Luke 4:29)! We ourselves get jolted, even shocked, when we realize his words were meant not just for his own kind but for all times and cultures, and most relevantly, our own. The compelling questions, then, for our reflection are: Do we let in his words for our consideration? Will we ponder this critical message of Jesus? Do we let his words challenge, maybe convict us, personally and as a culture? Or do we rationalize, get defensive, and consider his words applicable only to others? Might our reaction be just a quick thought, followed by a hasty dismissal and a return to our normal routines?

In our times and in every age, so many people, God's very children who are invited to live in God's love, waste much of their lives spiritually blind, deaf, and lame; poor, afflicted, and brokenhearted, just as Isaiah 61:1–3 describes. This plight is comparable to the people of 250 years before Christ, as described by Plato in his dialogue, *The Republic*[1]: living in underground shadows of reality rather than above ground in the light of truth and hope. I am also reminded of the comment of the American essayist, Henry David Thoreau (d. 1862), concerning many of his contemporaries: that "the mass

---

1. See Plato, *Republic,* 1–277.

of men lead lives of quiet desperation."[2] Jesus' pronouncement of Isaiah's words is equally challenging, saying he has come to awaken us to a freer, happier life, but only if we are "poor enough" to receive the Good News (Isa 61:1); that is, if we are humble and honest about our shortcomings. Teresa, like Jesus, asserts we must face these truths with a willingness to bear with and grow through the crosses of our life.

Jesus challenged the Nazarenes, as he did the rich young man, to choose whether they really wanted to be free and alive in God. This invitation required examining how unfree they were and recognizing how some of their values and attitudes were preventing them from being free and truly happy. Jesus came to "proclaim liberty to captives" and an "opening of the prisons to those who are bound . . . [a] year of the Lord's favor . . . to comfort all who mourn . . . to give them a garland instead of ashes, the oil of gladness instead of mourning, the mantle of praise instead of a faint spirit," [so] that they would be "oaks of righteousness, the planting of the Lord" (Isa 61:1–3). In Jesus, God would be the Way, the Truth, and the Life for us (John 14:6).

The challenge and awesome promises of Jesus have been proclaimed to every generation since then, and to each of us today. But, how do his words affect us? Do we truly want a deeper life and friendship with him, even unto a total surrender? Or are we, like the rich young man, caught between conflicting desires? For our asking, God's grace will eventually awaken us to the core of our soul and evoke our best and deepest desires. He will empower us to choose this new freedom on two conditions: first, we must be willing to work closely with him when facing the obstacles to our deeper desires, turning our lives over to God; second, we need to embrace the Father's will for us, realized through our following the guiding hand of his Holy Spirit.

PERSONAL FACTORS INHIBITING FAITH

Michael Paul Gallagher, in his *Free to Believe: Ten Steps to Faith,* presents at length four kinds of obstacles to our belief in Jesus and his way: personal, cultural, rigid thinking, and skewed perceptions. The first kind are personal factors that can greatly hinder us in our response to the call of Jesus. Gallagher cites the need to become aware of certain blind spots, self-promoting attachments, idols, and traps in our thinking if we are to grow spiritually.

2. Thoreau, *Walden*, 7.

Does this not imply what Teresa of Avila insists on: self-knowledge? We need to know the parts of ourselves that prevent our responding with faith and trust in God, as well as have the will to overcome them. We do not want to emulate the Israelites who wanted to return to Pharaoh's Egypt, to the familiar, the guaranteed, and the comfortable, when their journey to freedom through the desert became long and arduous. We can choose a freedom God so desires to give us, or settle for only a fraction of our God-given possibilities.

Gallagher notes common blocks to realizing a healthy relationship with God and how faith and trust in God begin to grow. Much depends on our gaining some understanding regarding the issues that anesthetize, so to speak, our hearts. With such insights we most likely will feel a new hope and reach out in prayer to Jesus for healing and guidance. Good pastoral leadership and praxis need to appreciate this, that challenges to our believing demand more than just information about our Christian faith (i.e., programs that emphasize apologetics). The struggles of people, Gallagher says,[3] are much more often problems with self-truth and our needs for healing hurtful memories, for forgiveness, and for being freed from guilt and shame. It often involves the search for self-worth and the courage to embrace our self, to be myself. These are issues that are truly spiritual in nature. Frequently the search for God and deeper faith encompasses the whole life cycle: needing to process experiences related to our family of origin, adolescence, midlife issues, or our aging and mortality. Growth in our life with God might require opening up about what so far has been unresolved: feelings of a poor self-image, anger issues, struggles with our sexuality, or learning to maintain our peace while under authority figures, to name a few.

For a long time we might not be ready to wrestle with such challenging parts of ourselves, but eventually, by the grace of God, we find the will to want to be free and are ready to face these crosses in our life. Possible obstacles to faith, hope, and love, derived from Gallagher and my own experience, are listed below.

3. See Gallagher, *Free to Believe*, 3.

PERSONAL OBSTACLES

1. Suffering from deep hurts: verbal, physical, or sexual abuse. Coming from a home life with little personal affirmation but receiving much criticism, being shamed, neglected.

2. Not experiencing myself as worthwhile; having a weak sense of personal identity, struggling to trust myself and others. Lonely, with little ability to enter significant friendships.

3. Defining myself in terms of the culture's definitions of success and failure vis-à-vis possessions and money, titles, and public recognition. One-sided lifestyle: identifying with work, studies, etc.; driven by fear of failing in my work/career/marriage. Weak or no sense of vocation, of God's offer of purpose/mission in life, of friendship and guidance.

4. Envying and being resentful toward others more successful than me and having more than I do.

5. Carrying an attitude of entitlement, worshiping the ideal me as an individual in control of my life; weak sense of gratitude, respect, or taste for anything spiritual.

6. Living with undue curiosity about what is immediate and entertaining; a weak sense of long-range purpose. Having little sense of wonder in nature, in the stars and heavens, in people; largely blind to or lacking appreciation of much of what is good, true, and beautiful. Slothful.

7. Experiencing religion as just dogmatic statements, moral warnings, and with no sense of connecting personally with God; settling for a conventional form of religion.[4] Identifying church with God.

These personal obstacles can become entrenched over the years and significantly hinder our spiritual growth. We may settle for a life partially conscious and shallow. Until we can name whatever the obstacles are and cooperate with God's grace to escape their hold on us, we will not come to mature faith in God. Jesus frequently says if we are to live a life worth living (Luke 9:23–25), we must engage our own personal humanity and do battle with our own selves. This might include admitting to certain truths about ourselves and past mistakes we are ashamed of. Gallagher claims we must

---

4. See Gallagher, *Free to Believe*, 13–27. Some examples are from Gallagher; most are my own.

"first find [our]false self and then [we] will have some chance of discovering [our] true self."[5]

We must work with our truth, then, both its positive aspects and its humbling parts. Growth in faith, otherwise, is minimal if at all, when our false self controls our thinking and feeling. It will squelch our deeper thirst and bury our inner, deeper self (Eph 3:16). Is not Gallagher's point what the Twelve-Step process of Alcoholics Anonymous and other substance-recovery programs insist on for their participants? Many others find the help they need from Jesus' Spirit through prayer, through spiritual reading, and through the spiritual guidance of a person rooted in God's Spirit and having good psychological wisdom.

CULTURAL OBSTACLES

Gallagher writes powerfully about how our culture influences us for better or for worse in how we live with ourselves, with our neighbor, and with God, if at all.[6] We may live in a nation with a repressive culture where allegiance to a dictator's ideology supplants any spiritual commitment. This situation will challenge our fidelity to God, to what is loving in our family, and to our own conscience. Even in a repressive culture, however, there remains a choice. We can either succumb as mindless citizens to this coercion, or courageously face the oppression and move beyond our fears toward God.

Many of us in the Western world, on the other hand, find ourselves to be unduly impacted by a consumerist ideology with its huge web of advertising, buying, and identifying with the things we own and consume. It pushes us to a pace of life that is so busy and allows little or no time for reflection. Much of this scenario is described in chapter 1. We get evangelized with an alternative gospel that encourages a very distorted sense of freedom for the individual to do whatever seems good. It promises happiness and comfort but delivers nothing more than what has been called "globalized superficiality"[7] (i.e., superficiality of thought, vision, dreams, relationships, and convictions). That is because one's "perception of the good is obscured by our prejudices, wishful thinking, and unruly desires; this perception changes constantly [since] different things appeal to different parts of our

---

5. See Gallagher, *Free to Believe*, 13.

6. See Gallagher, *Free to Believe,* 28–41.

7. See Nicolas, "Depth, Universality, and Learned Ministry," 2–3.

divided selves."[8] Over time, this way of living can lead to an abiding restlessness, an urgent search for meaning. Their state of soul could be described as one of spiritual anorexia. Like some alcoholics, we can eventually be pained enough to seek a way out of what is suffocating our spirit, like someone frantically coming up for air after being underwater for so long.

A side effect of this implicitly atheistic affluence, and a further insight as to why faith does not grow among many, is the failure of some first-world people to appreciate the huge disparity between their very comfortable world and much of the rest of the world. They are blind to systems of unjust consumption and overindulging wealth that keep billions of the world's peoples locked in grinding, dehumanizing poverty. This leaves them not caring about such people and insulating themselves from the cries of the poor. Sometimes religion is coopted to justify this lifestyle as God's reward to his hard-working, covenanted people. Choosing to ignore this fact of such egregious, scandalous disparity is the same kind of choice the rich man makes in Luke 16:19–31: ignoring Lazarus, the poor beggar lying just outside his house gate and covered in sores that dogs lick. People who live this kind of asocial, distorted, "Jesus and me" religion do not know Jesus nor the God of Jesus. Their faith is in a God who exists only in their falsely informed, ideologically brainwashed minds.

OBSTACLES DUE TO RIGID, NARROW THINKING

An additional obstacle to faith is the habit of applying the scientific method to the realm of personal relationships, including one's relationship with God.[9] What is real for these people is the factual and verifiable. Only what is empirical and admits of measurement and deductive reasoning is real knowledge; the intuitive way of knowing is at best approximate and lacks sufficient objectivity. Such people practically reject any other way for acquiring truth. Their mindset shuts off their sense of wonder and beauty, making their spiritual hunger and God's revelation almost impossible to recognize. Superiority, the need for control, and sometimes cynicism shape their stance toward life. God is unreal to them or quite distant; often he is explained away as a projection by people who lack courage to deal decisively with their lives. Many people, especially impressionable youth, can

---

8. Sparough et al., *What's Your Decision?*, 149.
9. See Gallagher, *Free to Believe*, 28–41.

get misdirected by such arguments that reject different kinds of knowledge and ways to truth. Sadly, this can greatly hinder their faith life.

This kind of narrow thinking and its prejudice for only the empirical, to the exclusion of faith in God, is embraced by those convinced that hope for the world is found in what the human person can accomplish through science and technology. For them it is not faith in God but humanity and its ingenious applications in physics, chemistry, biology, astronomy, aeronautics, etc., that will assure the future of the world. So, too, the internet and its seemingly infinite possibilities has opened us up to a fascinating, much better, and previously unimaginable world. Who needs God, then, when one is convinced that human beings using technology and science constitute the real god and are the ultimate source of the world's hopes and future?

OBSTACLES DUE TO SKEWED PERCEPTIONS

Lastly, the images of God we form, especially from our family of origin and early religious formation, have a great influence on whether our faith life grows or is significantly crippled. Gallagher presents an extensive list of distorted images of God.[10] He mentions the following: God is seen as

1. a detached watchmaker; a vague, distant force, not very caring or interested in us;

2. a moody god, like a flawed member of the clergy: bossy, cranky, moody, peevish, fussy;

3. a god who likes what we never like; a kill-joy, puritanical;

4. a solemn bore, pompous;

5. a big bully god, hostile and judgmental;

6. a torturing god who corresponds to images of hell running deep in our primitive selves;

7. a vengeful, punitive god; all tragedies or accidents are punishments for our sins;

8. the miracle worker of spectacular magic; yet, why is this god not preventing suffering?;

9. the god-who-did not-give-what-I-asked-for;

10. See Gallagher, *Free to Believe*, 42–50.

10. a security-blanket god; a puppeteer who micromanages our lives;

11. or a god who is a jealous competitor, sulky when we get busy with our lives.

Images of God can be influenced by our vulnerability and hypersensitivity, by our projections of inferiority or superiority, or from a literal understanding of metaphorical religious language.[11] If we are to grow beyond the third dwelling places, i.e., beyond a "church-reliant faith" to a personally appropriated "faith-as-decision,"[12] we must get beyond these misperceptions and experience the true God, who is love beyond mere human understanding.

Sadly, many people do not get beyond these four kinds of obstacles because, as St. John of the Cross points out, they seek guidance from people who purport to understand the world of spirit but who in fact do not. Often these so-called guides ignore or repudiate the teachings of Jesus regarding the cross.[13] Their counsel comes from some caricature or rationalization of what is essentially spiritual. Then, too, many needing help cannot trust nor be led beyond their past. They rely on what worked at earlier stages of prayer and mission. Or they live among those who hardly model the life of a true disciple of Jesus. Then there are some people who are simply not very reflective or insightful.

Nothing blocks faith, however, more than our own habitual sinful behaviors, values, and attitudes, especially the refusal to forgive our neighbor or ourselves. These sinful ways underlie the obstacles to faith listed above and require radical healings through God's truth and mercy.

In the history of the human family, the primary mistake or sin has been people's attempts to be God. We often seek ultimate control and independence. We implicitly, sometimes explicitly, deny our dependence on God and build our own world according to inflated images of ourselves. This is to make God in *our* image and likeness! It is to indulge human pride that blocks seeing our limitations, our woundedness too, and fosters a certain coldness of heart and weak faith in God.

It is a cross for us to face our truth, its vulnerabilities and needs, and ultimately our mortality. Jesus insists there is very little life with him and personal growth except through our wrestling with these humbling

---

11. See Gallagher, *Free to Believe*, 54–55.

12. See Gallagher, *Free to Believe*, 57.

13. See John of the Cross, *The Living Flame of Love,* Stanza III, secs. 54–62.

realities. It is *the* way of God to a fullness of life here and in the next, and St. Paul admits it is a "stumbling block to the Jews and folly to Gentiles, but to those who are called, . . . Christ the power and the wisdom of God" (1 Cor 1:23). Elsewhere, he says so forcefully: God's strength is encountered not in spite of, but precisely in and through, these weaknesses of ours (2 Cor 12:9–10). How counter-cultural!

Consider how Adam and Eve were guilty of this fundamental sin of wanting to be as gods (Gen 3:1–7). Their sin was preceded by the sin of some of the angels of God who, out of envy (Wis 2:24; Isa 14:12–15), wanted to be as God; they rebelled and fell from their glorious state. When we look at the sins of the more notorious and consider the deeper layers of their motivation, we keep returning to the same basic insight: we sin, we build our own Tower of Babel (Gen 11:1–9) and false kingdom, to give ourselves a sense of self-sufficiency, of being in control and feeling superior. This describes a caricature of the real God, who is so humble in his manner with us. Thankfully, God, in his mercy, resists all ways in which we might relate out of pride and from any desire to dominate others.

A frequent expression of the very nature of sin, then, is our refusal to accept ourselves as we are. There is a core sense of separation and alienation of our self from our truth or true self.[14] We often do not like the self we find inside (e.g., our feeling burdened with one or more of the obstacles mentioned above); we want to be someone else, and so we go searching restlessly for a better, greater self, a self on our terms and the world's, not on God's terms. This is our core disorder, our root sin. Before it is an action, it is a condition or state of wounded existence that our sinful actions express.[15] This condition of our self being separated from our true self leads us, then, to a sense of separation and alienation from our neighbor and from God. It is the prime obstacle to growth in the God-life, more basic than any other obstacle named in this chapter.

The antidote to these obstacles is to trust God and surrender to his will for us, to grow into the freedoms that come from being a close friend of God and a Beloved Disciple of Jesus. This trust is exactly what Jesus challenged his fellow Nazarenes to engage in, addressed in the closing parts of chapter 3, and challenges us to engage in as well. It is our choice to trust or not trust, to surrender or to cling to controlling our lives and futures. Healthy spiritual growth depends on this foundational sense of trust: trusting God

14. See Tillich, "You Are Accepted," 153.
15. See Tillich, "You Are Accepted," 154.

and life as good and, despite all sufferings, as ultimately benevolent or loving. Men and women need to pass through this crucial developmental stage in their own distinctive ways. Authentic relationships with God, self, and others require this trust in God's love and acceptance of us as we are. Only then will they have a self they can value enough and feel confident about when giving themselves to other human beings and to God.

Our being healed of this core disorder of not trusting God but rather our own selves and being reeducated in the ways of Jesus will be the focus of our next chapter. It will address the battle between what is frequently referred to as our true self and false self, with the struggle to face personal truths that humble our inflated egos. Hopefully, we will eventually come to appreciate why we all need a Savior. Jesus, whose name means "God saves," is the only way out of this state of spiritual powerlessness with its many temptations to try to save ourselves (Rom 7:14–25, especially v. 25).

QUESTIONS FOR DISCUSSION AND FAITH-SHARING

- Can you recognize yourself in any of Gallagher's descriptions of the four kinds of obstacles to faith in God? What helped you overcome one or other of these obstacles? How much was your prayer a determining factor in your making progress in becoming more free to believe?

- Are you surprised to learn that the refusal to be self-accepting, that giving in to being envious of others and trying to earn security, esteem, and affection, is the root cause of all sins? If you disagree with this point, what would you think is the root of all the world's troubles, of the sins of humanity? Do you find any of the struggles for self-acceptance stirring in you? Was there a time in your life when you were more subject to that temptation than now? What was that like?

- Do you think certain obstacles named by Gallagher are likely to affect men more than women? And some more likely to affect women than men? Which ones?

- Which obstacles seem to affect your children or students or fellow workers the most? Has it dissuaded them from being churchgoers or not? If so, have they overcome such obstacles and returned to an active life of worship in the church?

5

Learning to Surrender Control and Trust God

AN IMPORTANT CAUTION

IN THIS CHAPTER I describe the major shift in our life that is needed in order to grow beyond the third dwelling places. This major conversion relies much more on the initiatives of God than on our own efforts. We need, then, to learn how to relate in a new way to God, to self, to neighbor, and to the gift of life.

After reading the previous two chapters, we may feel eager to take whatever action is necessary and to accelerate this process of transformation into a much richer life in God. This attitude is usually a carryover from the ways we learned to relate in the first three dwelling places. Just to desire this deepening in our life with God is itself a significant grace of God. It is part of a call or vocation, like what happened to the prophets and wisdom figures in the Hebrew Scriptures when they were called. However, lest we approach this challenge and opportunity as something we are determined to make happen, we need above all to remember that it is God who guides and empowers our way along this new way of living and grants the freedoms available in the fourth dwelling places and beyond. It would be a major mistake if we give greater trust to our own judgments and determined strength than to God's Spirit when hoping for the wonderful blessings of the latter dwelling places. We can get into making our own plans to effect this transformation, get ahead of God and his guidance, and waste a huge opportunity. We must learn to listen, then, much more closely to God and allow him to lead. We are to be schooled in how to love much more deeply and live with greater passion this precious life we are being given. What a call! What a destiny!

I have already noted how as creatures of habit, and especially for those in the third dwelling places, we can succumb to complacency in our relationship with God and grow very little. I mentioned that Teresa of Avila five centuries ago lamented the same phenomenon in her times. The same was true for Jesus in his days. The story of the rich young man he met is timeless in its application. Throughout history we witness the perennial temptation to avoid looking at where we need conversion and healing. We are tempted by our fears and desires for security and affection; we allow our desire for esteem, through disordered attachments to persons and our plans for our future, to subvert our deeper desires. Too often we try to guarantee our own sense of happiness, fulfillment and, implicitly, our self-designed salvation.

Jesus spoke to this self-defeating way of living by encouraging us to be open to the Spirit of his loving Father in each present moment. He urges us to entrust ourselves to the power of this Spirit and experience for ourselves how real and close God is with his providential care: "Fear not, little flock, for it is your Father's good pleasure to give you the kingdom" (Luke 12:32). The kingdom is not just a future event, a far-off-in-the-future climax to history, but is also God's powerful, loving *presence*, right here, right now: a dynamic, benevolent, and guiding power inside us and among the people around us. God is the underground River of Divine Life uniting the almost 8 billion of us now on the earth, animating and gathering us into a new and everlasting family. We will know the power of this invitation only by experiencing it, by trusting God enough to try to live in him. We need only to ask the Holy Spirit for faith and courage to walk in the Way of Jesus.

In every now for the asking, then, God is available to enlighten and guide us. He calls us to reform, to be purified, and with the help of his Spirit to dare to live as Jesus did when he walked among us. Instead of wasting our lives on what cannot satisfy our search for meaning and happiness, the Holy Spirit will lead us—if we will permit, *if we will ask*—into the freedom, joy, and fulfillment we have been made for.

AGAIN, THE BIGGEST OBSTACLE TO THIS CALL

We soon learn when we try to respond to this call that we must begin to entrust everything to God, in the fourth dwelling places and beyond. This lesson, sometimes painful but always freeing, is a prerequisite for any significant conversion to the wisdom of Jesus' ways, to a deeper, more vibrant life in the Holy Spirit. Perhaps we must make numerous mistakes regarding this matter in order not to make those mistakes. We need to fail and be humbled often in trying to save ourselves before we finally learn that this is not the Way of Jesus.

The journey through the first two dwelling places demands significant effort on our part to respond to the helping hand of God, to escape the spiritual quagmire we have been living in, and to arrive at the third stage. Whether our keeping the commandments, as Teresa says is often the mark of people in the third dwelling places, or simply living what we would call a basically good and moral life, either way can seem so much the result of our own efforts. We can be like some of the Pharisees of Jesus' time and like disciples of the fifth-century Irish monk Pelagius (d. 420), who taught that if we put our minds with determination to any moral challenge, we can bring ourselves to obey God's command.[1] After that, God's grace will reward us. We can look at our mental, analytical, artistic, planning, and money-making gifts and abilities, and it becomes easy to think these are all things we are initiating and achieving. We then miss recognizing how all of this originates as a gift from God, to be used with God for creating something great, greater than what we could ever do on our own.

We do not appreciate how futile it is to live with this attitude of trying to be our own savior, our own source of strength and growth, until we seek greater growth in Christ. We will experience how it is even counterproductive to the realization of our deeper desires. Growth is divinely evoked, not self-initiated. Spiritual growth is a gift we must be humble enough to ask for again and again and learn how to receive.

Eventually life teaches us, and grace is given to us, to acknowledge that everything is a gift, that we need God's grace more than we did in the first three dwelling places if we are to grow into the later stages. Those in the third dwelling places who humbly seek the self-knowledge that Teresa of Avila insists on for further growth begin to experience what I call a spiritual Copernican revolution.

---

1. Hellwig, *Understanding Catholicism*, 163–65.

THE GREAT REVERSAL

For the earliest centuries human beings were convinced that the sun revolved around the earth and that our world was the center of everything. In the sixteenth century, however, the astronomer Copernicus (d. 1543) discovered that the relationship of the earth to the sun is just the opposite. Similarly, there comes a time when those living in the third dwelling places are given by God a beginner's understanding of the true relationship of ourselves to him. Evolving from living as the center and God as the satellite, they learn through experience that God, not one's self, is the center of the human spirit and lives in our deepest self. This is truly a new way of thinking and relating; it will have to be reinforced by many experiences to become one's habitual way of relating to God and to one's own self.

This revolution in understanding and integrating into our life this much more authentic way of relating to God has enormously important implications for how we live the rest of our life. It is fascinating to see the growth that happens once we accept this saving truth and live with greater fidelity toward God: fidelity to God as God is, and to ourselves as we are, and to neighbor and all other parts of creation as they are. We need to learn to accept life on God's terms, not ours. Otherwise, we live as though we are God.

BEING LOVED, HUMBLED, AND SET FREE

What, then, will free us from this widespread distorted way of regarding our self, our life with God and neighbor, and help us escape the limits of the third dwelling places? It will be a *deeper, more personal experience of God.* St. John of the Cross says that God does this by attracting us beyond our familiar pleasures and habits to something more lovable, to what is more pure and worthy of what we have been made for.[2] Teresa talks about this in terms of our coming to experience Jesus as a very dear friend. Friendship with him that soon grows into a strong love will draw us in.

Specifically, God, Abba Father, reveals Jesus to us. We awaken to how Jesus is more attractive and worthy of our love than all the people, possessions, memories, and customs of our life. This awareness is a gift of God that the rich young man was not open to, not able to take in at that time.

---

2. See John of the Cross, *Ascent of Mount Carmel*, bk. I, ch. 13, secs. 3 & 4, ch. 14, sec. 2. Hereafter, *Ascent*, I, 13, 3 & 4; 14, 2.

In other words, we are blessed to encounter Jesus in prayer in the Gospels as a greater love than our previously disordered loves. We might also experience him and his Holy Spirit in a community we belong to (e.g., in Bible study, Lectio Divina, group charismatic-style prayer, or in family life, our work world, or in outreach to the poor). We can meet him in so many different settings and be strongly impacted by his person, goodness, and lovable manner; by his truth and especially by his merciful acceptance of us and others as we are. The eyes of our heart open and we meet Jesus as never before: alive right now and so personal. These kinds of encounters give rise to desires deeper than we had previously experienced and can move us quite powerfully to give our love in return and allow ourselves to be guided.

What can also move us to a closer life with God are situations like losing control over our health; becoming terminally ill; memories of past moral failures; financial disaster and the humiliation and fears that go with it. Such experiences can often be painful; they get our attention, but, praise God, they can open us up to the real God and to a more honest, humble way of relating to ourselves. Suffering through events like these, perhaps experiencing a collapse of life as we knew it, can open us to meeting Jesus as our refuge, as our Savior, more personal than ever.

Other less dramatic examples can be realizing we are too responsible or controlling; more jealous or impatient than we thought; judgmental toward others; prone to self-pity and gossip; or lacking in compassion at times.[3] We might discover we suffer from a fear of not being that loveable and hide behind a mask of saintly humility. Or we experience disillusionment with a marriage partner, child, relative, work colleague, or a public figure we have held in high esteem, and this spurs us to be open and vulnerable with God and discover how much we need Jesus in our life.[4]

What is essential to know at this point is that God can capitalize on these not-so-rare experiences of our crosses, humiliations, and sufferings, bring us closer to our truth, and let us receive new freedoms, while appreciating more than ever our great need for him. They can be instruments by which God gradually effects a reversal of our realizing him as our true center. He accomplishes this miracle of transformation through loving attraction, not by force.

3. In naming many of these obstacles here and in chapter 6, I am indebted to Sr. Mary Niere, who mentions them in her *The Gospel of Contemplation*. She cites them as instances of our experiencing God allowing us to be humbled through our fragile humanity and giving us an opportunity to come closer to him.

4. Niere, *Gospel of Contemplation*, 1–55.

PRAYER: THE MEANS TO OUR GROWTH

This revolution in our life can also involve major changes in the way we pray. Often those who are called out of the third dwelling places have been blessed to do so by having been faithful over some years to regular personal prayer focused principally on Jesus. They have meditated on the life of Jesus and been moved to imitate and love him. With the help of their imagination, they have entered the scenes of the Gospels and become engaged in their stories as applicable to themselves. Their hearts and minds have been formed by personally engaging Jesus as teacher, visionary, healer, and especially as friend. They experience a growing affection for him and a deeper understanding of his Way. They are attracted to becoming his disciple and are moved to offer their heart and life to him. This kind of prayer is commonly referred to as discursive meditation. But in time they can be moved toward greater simplicity, less mental and imaginative activity, and longer periods of quiet. Teresa of Avila calls this second way of prayer "active recollection,"[5] a kind of nondiscursive centering prayer we can attain by our own efforts.

Then there can come a time when God mysteriously draws such people even closer to him through a more passive or receptive form of prayer that is truly supernatural in origin, not acquired by our own efforts, and which is deeper than active recollection.[6] It is commonly called "the prayer of quiet," which is the initial stage of contemplative prayer. Teresa says, "one noticeably senses a gentle drawing inward . . . it doesn't come when we want it but when God wants to grant us the favor."[7] She adds that God calls such people "especially to be attentive to interior matters . . . so that [their] soul instead of striving to engage in discourse strives to remain attentive and aware of what the Lord is working in it."[8] Those called in this way will feel inclined to greater quiet and no words.

God initiates this deeper way of prayer by letting us experience a certain waning of interest in the usual ways of meditating and then by a drying up of the felt consolations previously experienced so readily. In its beginnings we can feel lost and without guidance, possibly afraid that we have made a mistake in our relationship with God. We can be tempted to go back to our

5. *IC*, IV, 3, 1.
6. *IC*, IV, 3, 3 & 3, 4.
7. *IC*, IV, 3, 3.
8. *IC*, IV, 3, 3 & 3, 4.

more familiar ways of praying. With competent guidance by a spiritually knowledgeable person and/or books on prayer we will more likely recognize the way of light and truth in these new experiences, despite what often feels confusing, and trust that God is gently and lovingly leading us.[9]

During this time of transition, we learn to be more still in our body and mind, more steadily attentive to God and only God, and with eyes gently closed, to rest in him. We learn to stop doing and *just be*, while gently focusing off any memories, feelings, thoughts, images, or any sudden insight or intuition; refraining from saying anything beyond the reciting of a mantra or prayer-word. We discover the depths of such prayer when simply *gazing with love* at God (not at an image of God but resting steadily in an intuited sense of God being right here) and sometimes—during prayer or outside that time—find welling up from our depths intense desires to pour out our whole being to God. We recognize firsthand how close is the underground River of Divine Life, the Spirit of the risen Christ moving through us. It can be a very powerful way of experiencing God as never before, of how intimate God and we can be with each other.

These deeper desires are manifestations of divine love "capturing" us (Jer 20:7–9), leading us to a new life far beyond what we could have anticipated or even known to ask for (Eph 3:20 and 1 Cor 2:9). Experiences of loss and confusion, whether in prayer or daily life, are moments of facing our human limitations. These occasions, in the hands of God, greatly expanding our spiritual capacities, evoke deeper desires in us and empower us with new freedoms (2 Cor 12:7–10).

The challenges presented above to our self-protected, customary ways of living and praying can be understood as part of what John of the Cross calls the dark night of our soul. They make us face the difficult, painful parts of reality: namely, the fact that as humans we are quite limited and need God to make any progress. They are struggles that can bring us into the presence of a God who can liberate us, for example, from fear, greed, and the foolishness of trying to live as though we can manage our daily affairs and provide for ourselves. Either we try to hide from these humbling realities and deny their meaning, or we learn from them. If we are too afraid, stubborn, smug, or lazy to face these parts of ourselves, and if

---

9. Some books which have been helpful in my appreciating the riches of contemplative prayer are: Green, *When the Well Runs Dry*; many profound writings of John Main; the fourteenth-century classic, *The Cloud of Unknowing* (esp. 156–66); and Boase, *Prayer of Faith*. Also: Laird, *Into the Silent Land*; many writings of Thomas Keating; and Jalics, *Called to Share in HIS Life*. Finally, Seelaus, *Distractions in Prayer*.

we do not ask for some wise guidance, then we will stay stuck in these third dwelling places all our lives. Perhaps we will still lead a good Christian life but fail to grow into a loving friendship with Jesus and Abba Father.

What is so important to appreciate about this process of our becoming centered in God is how it is God, not ourselves or any other creature, whether through joy or pain, through peak encounters or in losses, who moves us to this new relationship. God alone empowers us to live more from the great underground River of Divine Life, with genuine, humble love and the habit of entrusting everything to him.

There follow two examples of people undergoing this major transformation in life.

BEING TRANSFORMED: AN EXAMPLE

Jerry is in his early forties, has been married sixteen years, and is the father of four children, the oldest being nearly fifteen. He has worked long and hard at a mid-level management position in an auto parts factory. College education costs are imminent expenses. Over the last two years he has been expecting a promotion with a significant pay raise, yet has witnessed others, younger and with less seniority, being promoted ahead of him. He feels a certain injustice. He could represent his situation to top-level management and risk being marked as pushy, or hang on and keep his discontent to himself while hoping against hope that he still might be promoted. The present job market is not at all promising. At home he is eating more than usual, gaining weight and not exercising as he once did. He relaxes most evenings by watching TV, snacking and drinking two glasses of wine. He feels mildly depressed and less attentive to his wife and children.

Evan, one of his best friends and fellow workers, mentions to Jerry that he is concerned for him because of his moods; noting he is not exercising as before, is no longer upbeat, and not very present to others at work. Jerry is shaken by what Evan says and knows he needs to take his friend's concern to heart. Helped by some readings Evan tells him about concening the spirituality of surrender and trust in God, Jerry begins to feel a certain letting go happening inside with an inspiration to entrust to God the future needs, educational and otherwise, of his children. So, too, with respect to his work, he might get a promotion and a significant pay increase; but again, he might not. What has shifted for Jerry is his entrusting to God the future of both his children and his job situation.

In fact, he senses he is being invited to allow God more room in all aspects of his family's future, his marriage, and his own life, and to trust that whatever the true needs of each family member, God will provide. Letting go of closely managing the future of his children to assure their turning out a certain way and surrendering his job situation ultimately to God are big steps forward for Jerry. "I am getting out of the boat on these issues and walking on water," he exclaims (Matt 14:28–29).

This inner shift of attitude is a conversion moment for him, a Copernican event; it is a time when he is to let go of needing to be in control, to be everything in providing for his family members and be more open with his wife and God about his feelings. His experience of personal powerlessness and allowing God to lead them all into the future changes his relationship with God and the way he understands himself as husband and father. His is anything but an attitude of irresponsible apathy, of abdicating responsibility.

As he lets go, thanks to his spiritual reading and regular practice of what is described above as active recollection or centering prayer, Jerry says, "I have been feeling a consolation and peace I never knew before." He is like his old self again, but better. A certain joy along with desires to get closer to God and family well up within him at various times. He is attracted to things more interesting than watching evening TV and numbing himself with wine. Jerry knows he is being guided. God's personal care for him has become more real. He can now relate to the saying, "let go and let God" while still being involved as father and role-model in his family.

ANOTHER EXAMPLE OF TRANSFORMATION

Emmy Lou, a widow for many years, lives in a badly maintained house in a dangerous part of the city where at night there are occasional break-ins, stickups, assaults, and murders. Her three children are now in their late twenties and early thirties. One son has a serious issue with drugs and is usually unemployed. A second one is doing time at a federal prison for carjacking. Her only daughter is living with a boyfriend and two little ones fathered by her former live-in partner.

Life, then, is tough for Emmy Lou. She stays steady, however, saying:

> I don't know what I would do without my church friends. I love to pray and sing with them. But more so, the Bible is precious to me. I find so much strength there; the Lord always gives me the Word I need for the day. I have put my family and my life in his hands.

> There is not much more I can do except love them as best I can the
> way they are. Jesus has taught me how to do this. When I pray, I
> don't think much anymore; I say very few words to him. Oh, I lift
> up to him my children's situations. But mostly, I just sit quiet. I
> "look" at him and he at me, and that's enough. We're fine this way
> together. We just love each other so much. He's my Rock, my all.

Then, after some silence, she looks down and slowly moves her head
from side to side and whispers, "But I feel such a longing . . . a *deep ache!*"
After a longer pause Emmy Lou exclaims, "Oh, my!" Quickly she looks
away with tears in her eyes and covers them with a hand. She is overcome
with joy at Jesus' love for her, at their closeness to each other, while at the
same time feeling the pain of her cross. She is being richly blessed through
the prayer of quiet.

IN CONCLUSION

This interior shift of focus, then, from our self as our center to welcoming
God as the center of our life marks the great crossover from the third to
the fourth dwelling places. It is the beginning of the Passover from enslavement in Egypt into the freedom of God's promised land. Jerry is learning to
make this shift of focus by facing his humbling reality, his limitations, and
finding God and God's strength in the midst of them. Emmy Lou learned
some time ago how to live and pray contemplatively and let God be God in
her life and family. The life-force or underground River of Divine Life welling up in their hearts is evident in their desires for a closer, more intimate
relationship with God.

It can then be understood from Jesus' proclamation in the synagogue
at Nazareth when reading Isaiah 61:1–3 that God is freeing them from
their demons of fear, discouragement, unbelief, and the temptation to fix
their situations through their own efforts. He is inviting them to live with
deep trust in him; in turn, God does this by attracting them to Jesus and
to himself as their Abba (John 17:3). Jerry and Emmy Lou are responding
beautifully to this invitation, being drawn to greater depths of relationship,
greater acceptance of themselves, and a greater share in God's joy, with a
freedom from fearing their crosses anymore. They are experiencing God in
unique and wonderfully freeing ways.

Once we consent to live this new way of welcoming God as our center
and adopt the basic disciplines of living more authentically, God proceeds

to clean our house of much of its clutter, of the false gods or idols which we have allowed into our lives. The Spirit of the risen Jesus begins now to work more vigorously in us, like an artist intent on sculpting something stunningly beautiful. Eventually he will eliminate any defect, every imperfection, and sees in us, at a distance, the quality and beauty of the final product, a new creation that only the divine Michelangelo could envision and effect. Our eventual beauty will be nothing less than that of Christ Jesus.

What specifically, then, does God work on to clean our house? This will be the focus of the next chapter.

QUESTIONS FOR DISCUSSION AND FAITH-SHARING

- Are you the type of person who tends to jump in and make this kind of conversion from self-centered, "I can do it" living to God-centered entrustment happen by extra efforts?

- Can you relate to the point of a growing friendship with Jesus, of coming to experience God as so beautiful and attractive and helping you undergo the spiritual Copernican revolution in your life, of letting go of former disordered loves and centering more in God/Jesus? Or might you relate to this conversion coming through your having to wrestle with one or more of the seven capital sins or the obstacles and challenges to faith and trust in God cited above? Share what you are willing to share.

- Have you experienced discursive meditation? Active recollection? The prayer of quiet? Share whatever you are willing to say, please, about these three ways of praying and the fruit borne from them.

- Have you met people like Ned and Emmy Lou? In what circumstances? What struck you the most about them?

6

Facing Our Sinfulness, Gaining Humbling Self-Knowledge

WHEN WE ARE WON over by God's loving initiatives the spiritual revolution referred to in the previous chapter begins to happen. We experience strong attractions to God, described by St. John of the Cross as "fired by love's urgent longings,"[1] and by St. Teresa in terms of being drawn into friendship with Jesus. God has been calling, healing, and purifying us throughout the first three dwelling places, but now—drawing us into the fourth set of dwelling places—God begins to take this process to a more radical level. We are now being readied to face some demanding inner work.

Major changes, described to some extent in the previous chapter, begin to take place in us, especially in our values. Experiencing Jesus, and the God he reveals as our greatest joy, attracts us, impels us to make a life-altering journey into God. More and more we fall in love with God as truly good and absolutely trustworthy, as worth our all. More authentic desires emerge in our consciousness, and well up more vigorously: in our prayer, in our daily living, in what we look for in relationships. These initiatives of God constitute a call for us to move toward a much deeper life with him while recognizing the ways we are not one with him.

---

1. See John of the Cross, *Ascent*, I, 11, 1–2.

It is neither our determination, then, nor our own efforts that effect this conversion. Instead, this new growth is effected by God asserting himself more in our hearts and empowering us to be more surrendered, more trusting, more available to his inspirations and call. The upper three levels of awareness—the sensuous, physical, and psychological of Diagram 1— are being permeated with many new inspirations in the Spirit to be purified of self-centered, sinful ways and be more given to God with a deeper love; God is transforming our hearts and minds in Christ.

The voice of Jesus challenges us to be more receptive to God, moving us to look inside, and if we consent, to show us where we can be freed. If we respond with humility and trust, we will in time experience soul-stretching desires. God will open our heart to new depths and reveal our deeper self, prompting longings for communion with the One who is more than we could have ever asked for or imagined (Eph 3:20). Such a process will involve more than just sweetness and consolation. Sometimes there will be longings and aching within, as happens to Emmy Lou in the previous chapter, because we experience God to be so good and generous, so beautiful in himself. We will desire to love with a love of which God is so worthy, while sensing how utterly inadequate we are out of our own poor means to love that much. In this holy unfolding of our soul's depths, the Spirit of God is recreating us. God does this not by suppressing or removing but by realigning the energies of our soul so that our choices are harmonized with his energies. The love that pours out of us, then, is so much greater than before. The resulting communion will sometimes feel like a taste of heaven.

Let us look in detail at what the Divine Doctor can free us from and for: a more authentic life and an unveiling of our inner core, our true spiritual identity. It is what the writer to the Ephesians in 3:16 calls *the inner man* (or hidden self) and in 4:24 refers to as *the new man* (or new self). This deepest self from which comes our most authentic desires or manifestations of *our life hidden with Christ in God* (Col 3:3) can be largely ignored and buried under the false gods we live for. They blind us to our inner God-given beauty and potential. Thankfully, the Holy Spirit will show us, if we are open to it, whatever is not in harmony with Christ and our true identity. The description of Jerry in the previous chapter illustrates this point. With the intervention and encouragement of his friend Evan, Jerry discovers, especially in his prayer, this new self or identity, his inner self anchored in the risen Christ. He is beginning to realize that he is part of a we; that he and the risen Christ Jesus share one life, Christ's divine life. This holy reality is the source of Jerry's strength to live free from fear and in fidelity to Christ and his own self (Gal 2:19b–20). Jerry is more his true self than ever, trusting the risen Christ to provide whatever he truly needs: in his work and in other important parts of his family's life, rather than resorting to depressants for relief from his burdens.

Listed below are different manifestations of the seven capital sins. More specifically, they are examples of the *roots* of these sins. They are the attitudes and values, unhealed memories and assumptions, some conscious and some unconscious, that underlie our behaviors and adversely influence our choices. They impact our thinking, weaken our will and heart/spirit, and even our body in some cases. This list cites ways we can run from facing and being healed of our personal hurts, wounds, and weaknesses. They also reflect elements of our culture that encourage self-focused living. Yes, there are so-called demons in us too, just as there were demons in the people of Jesus' day.

Our earthly journey will always involve wrestling with temptations and sometimes succumbing to sin. The wisdom of Christian spiritual maturity counsels us to be confident of God and at peace with this humbling truth that, till our death, we will always have something of these self-focusing dynamics active in us. Oftentimes our most significant growth in virtue comes when we are in a desolate state, tempted to sin, but we choose to resist these promptings of the self-centered self. To oppose them implies our choosing God and life with God rather than what these temptations are urging.

Let us now look at these various behaviors and attitudes, habitual perceptions that we might be carrying even from childhood. God enlightens us and calls us to release them to him for forgiveness and healing. In time we may be blessed to appreciate the core sin or disorder from which all our other sins spring up. It is then that we experience radical, major, life-giving reconciliation with God, with self, with neighbor, and with all creation.

ATTITUDES, VALUES, HABITS: ROOTS
OF THE SEVEN CAPITAL SINS

Pride: Manifested in . . .

1. Perfectionism; being unduly competitive, compulsive about succeeding; slow to admit mistakes and apologize; slow to forgive others and one's own self; legalistic about morality and church laws; scrupulous.[2]

2. Being largely focused on self with a poor sense of care for and interest in others; rarely complimenting or encouraging; often not thinking to say "thank you."

3. Not listening well, too ready to talk and dominate in groups. Argumentative. Having an undue need to tell others about their knowledge and successes.

4. Or being shy, quite self-conscious, slow to offer service or their own thoughts, overly sensitive because of fear of what others might think about them; little faith in God's love for them.

5. Being slow to share or give up control/power/authority; struggling to trust and accept direction from those in authority.

6. Thinking of their self-worth not in terms of God's love for them but largely in terms of their career, accomplishments, and money earned; influenced by an attitude of entitlement, of being the self-made successful man or woman.

7. Being deferential toward those with wealth, status, and titles; less attentive or caring toward others; seeking those in authority to agree with, to think well of them.

8. Being careless about people's reputations, prone to telling negative things about others; betraying confidences to get attention and feel important.

9. Taking a rationalistic approach to the spiritual life, trusting more in their reasoning powers than in God's Word and Divine Mystery; lukewarm, having a distant sense of God and little or no sense of the wonders of God's love.

10. Seeing themselves arriving at the third dwelling places largely through their own efforts; judgmental toward those struggling through the first two dwelling places and those outside their castle; ready to give spiritual advice beyond their limited experience and knowledge.[3]

---

2. I am indebted to Sr. Mary Niere and her *Gospel of Contemplation*, 13–17, for numerous examples listed under the headings of the seven capital sins.

3. For an in-depth analysis of pride, see Bergoglio (Pope Francis), *Way of Humility.*

Anger (i.e., anger that hurts self and others, not anger needing healthy expression):

1. Being impatient with others, with God, with self; being hot-tempered, critical, stubborn, jealous, moody, demanding of others. Very upset when the future threatens their control and stirs anxiety. Harsh toward themselves for past mistakes.

2. Not very forgiving; resentful, gossiping, and holding grudges.

3. Complaining to God about their own difficulties in life, in prayer; blame others, indulge in self-pity.

4. Holding racist, sexist, homophobic, or distorted religious attitudes and letting these attitudes influence their speech, actions, and how they vote.

5. Speaking uncharitably, unkindly, without compassion, even condemning those different from them; excluding the stranger or those judged as sinners and different.

6. Using God's name in disrespectful, irreverent, of even harsh ways. Enjoying violent movies and TV, feeding their imagination with scenes of anger, revenge, and violence.

Envy:

1. Disliking the person they have become so far. Not believing in God's love for them. Resenting and wanting what others own or have become so they might be more noticed, more successful.

2. Resenting others' goodness, progress, and recognition. Weak faith in God; not noticing God's ways of having loved them.

Avarice or Greed:

1. Undue desire for, and pursuit of, money, possessions, comfort, titles, success, and power over others. Invest in business ventures that ignore social impact on others, especially on children, health risks, and the ecosystem.

2. Wanting too much to be more secure, esteemed, recognized, praised, and envied.

3. Not sharing with those in need, especially with those who are poor/sick.

Lust:

1. Seeking sexual pleasure with themselves or others, outside marriage, through looks, fantasies, masturbation, and pornography, thereby "poisoning" their imagination and dividing their will between God and self-indulgence. Cohabiting before committing before God and church to one's beloved partner and to God.

2. Lacking respect for the other in the ways of expressing their sexuality. Living their sexuality exclusively for recreational purposes, not open to procreation when physically able and healthy enough to have children.

3. Indulging in fantasies that neither respect others nor their own self. Dressing in a seductive, alluring way, desiring to stimulate lustful thoughts and desires in others.

Sloth

1. Missing commitments or appointments because of disliking the efforts required.

2. Lacking the discipline needed for spiritual growth; lacking in ambition, hope, and courage. Timid, overly sensitive and cautious; skeptical, cynical, sarcastic.

3. Slacking off in prayer that does not reward them with felt consolations; avoid penance and fasting. Sleep too much.

4. Disregarding bodily care, engaging in little physical exercise. Do not heed their doctor's advice.

Gluttony

1. Seeking in prayer the consolations of God rather than God, whether in good times or difficult ones. Lack initiative; low self-confidence, compliant, moody.

2. Replacing God with their job, or indulging in much TV watching, too much food and alcoholic drink, entertainment, sports, drugs, internet involvement, twittering often about empty talk; spending a great amount of time on physical fitness, on personal appearance, etc.

Each of us has inclinations toward certain failings connected to the makeup of our personality, life experiences, and environment. It is these issues that we need to work on in union with the Holy Spirit. Those who do not acknowledge personal failings do not know God very well, or themselves, or their neighbor. They can rationalize their errant ways in terms of self-pity or entitlement and frustrate the Spirit's generous offer of conversion and freedom in Christ.

Teresa of Avila frequently emphasizes humility and self-knowledge as *the prerequisites* for any significant growth beyond the third dwelling places. This great truth might require our overcoming the fear of some loss; or letting go of the known and stepping into a very new situation or place; or relinquishing cherished ideas and the security found in past ways of doing things. It is our choice as to how we will respond to this challenging truth. Saying yes to what really is a divine invitation promises an expanded sense of our life, greater inner freedom, and the discovery of gifts we never knew we had.

THE NARROW GATE, THE WAY TO LIFE

In Matthew 7:13–14, Jesus describes two ways of living our life. One way is the easy way and is chosen by many, says Jesus; its gate is wide and leads to destruction. The other way is challenging and is chosen by few; its gate is narrow but leads to life. This critical juncture offers a choice: either settle into the habits and securities of the third dwelling places; or earnestly seek God as someone we truly want to know; desiring that we become close friends.

When we choose the wide road, we live mostly from the first three levels of awareness indicated in our first diagram. This does not necessarily imply sin, even though it readily exposes us to sin more than the courageous, generous choice of the narrow road. But it does indicate there is a noteworthy division of loyalties in our soul; God is not yet that personal and compelling for us. With our choosing the wide road goes a lesser capacity to feel deep joy, particularly the joy of God. So too our ability to enter into deep friendships and love with people. In general, our ability to appreciate what is good, true, and beautiful; what is unjust and needs to be challenged is proportionate to how deeply we experience God as the deepest desire of our desires.

But let us suppose that a deeper desire to live in and for God has arisen in our soul. Let us suppose that we have experienced such a blessing in one of two general ways, as was described in the previous chapter: either in the consolations of prayer and/or community; or in the humbling side of life, e.g., in the collapse of former securities and being visited with significant sufferings. We then need some strong directives on how to make the most of our situation and continue to grow in the Holy Spirit.

DIRECTIVE FOR CHOOSING JESUS' WAY

One of the more challenging and proven sets of directives in Christian asceticism comes from St. John of the Cross (d. 1591), what are called his precautions and counsels. They are anticipated in his *Ascent of Mount Carmel,* book I, chapter thirteen, and developed extensively in his *Collected Works.*[4] John stresses that for our spiritual growth, our will, or that part of us through which we make choices, is the most important of all the operations of our soul; more so than our sensing, reasoning, imagining, or remembering. It is with our will that we choose or reject God, choose our better self or lesser self. His counsels tell us what to do or avoid if we wish to grow significantly in intimacy with God. They make specific the advice St. Ignatius of Loyola gives in his *Spiritual Exercises,* paragraph 189, that growing in love for God requires our being freed more and more from disordered self-love, self-will, and self-interests,[5] so that in all our choices God, implicitly or explicitly, is our one and deepest choice.

John's counsels are clearly not for developing a self-sufficient personality.[6] Instead, our spiritual transformation must be the work of God, with

---

4. See John of the Cross, "Counsels," 662–65, and "Precautions," 656–61. There is appreciable overlap between John's Precautions and his Counsels. I treat the Counsels in the text above. Here I give a very abbreviated sense of the Precautions. First, the Precautions are warnings about three specific pitfalls preventing our experiencing the consoling peace of the Holy Spirit and union with God: undue attachments to creatures, deceits of the devil, and then our own selfish desires. They encourage us to focus not on any person, thing, or event as all-important, but to relate to any of them while at the same time remaining aware of and keeping a broader focus on Christ and Abba Father. This will keep us in balance by loving God first and then any creature in God. The Precautions, therefore, promote a wide-angle and in-depth faith consciousness as a gift of the Holy Spirit.

5. I acknowledge as useful and complementary of what John of the Cross teaches the insights of Thomas Keating concerning the false programs of happiness we can try to live out (seeking security, affection, and esteem) instead of seeking Christ as our healing and freedom. I have also found the enneagram personality test, with its nine personality types and three subtypes for each of the nine, to be clarifying of our various motives. It also gives us good examples of virtues, vices, and what conversion would look like in many instances.

6. Muto, *Words of Wisdom,* 61.

our role being that of cooperating with God. We are to "adapt . . . to God's self-communication through the theological virtues of faith, hope, and love."[7] These counsels, then, guide us in how to dispose ourselves to God's healing initiatives that open the door of our soul and let him, the Divine Doctor and Artist, accomplish the transformation that only he, in Christ, can achieve.

THE COUNSELS IN GENERAL

"The counsels presuppose that one has [already] undergone a deep conversion experience . . . a turning of our lives over to God."[8] In short, they assume we are living in the fourth or one of the later dwelling places. We feel the desire sometimes to be completely united with Jesus and the Father. The compelling attraction is to "abid[e] always in God's presence,"[9] so much do we experience God as our greatest joy and deepest desire. Such God-given longings energize our spirit to face whatever our calling requires, to embrace even a share in Jesus' passion. We are moved by a very great love that sometimes flames up inside us, as John of the Cross would say, impelling us to make choices and offer ourselves in ways far beyond what we had ever expected. This divinely initiated fire sustains us on our journey to pass through the narrow gate and travel the narrow road while confronting the ways we resist and fail. God, the love of our life, our joy as well as our anchor in dark times, will spur us on to learn from these falls and keep us hopeful regarding his promise of transformation in Christ.

THE BASIC PRINCIPLE: KNOW, LOVE, AND IMITATE JESUS

As something of an overarching principle to the counsels John of the Cross, like Teresa, stresses meditating regularly on Jesus in the Gospels; we must come to know, love, and imitate him if we are to grow into the latter dwelling places. It is in the steady fixing of our eyes on Jesus, on his person, his values, and his Way of living and dying, that the Holy Spirit opens us to our depths and changes our priorities dramatically (Phil 3:7–11). Like a

---

7. Kavanaugh, "Preface," 9.
8. Muto, *Words of Wisdom,* 60.
9. Muto, *Words of Wisdom,* 60.

powerful magnet, the goodness of Jesus and how lovable he is will draw forth the energies of our soul, concentrating them like a laser beam of previously scattered light rays. We begin to experience a burning in our soul to belong totally to God, to live and die for Christ Jesus, and to pour out ourselves for him in service of our neighbor as he did for me/us (Phil 2:1–11).

FOUR COUNSELS

John recommends four additional disciplines distinctive of the life of a committed follower of Jesus.[10] They are eminently practical in helping us overcome the tyranny of our ego, promoting wholeheartedness, and opening us to the deep joy of Christ.

FIRST COUNSEL: MONITOR CURIOSITY AND MAINTAIN INNER PEACE

Curiosity can be a way of opening us to new possibilities. But John cautions us to guard against undue curiosity, becoming too engaged in and preoccupied with the business of other people. Resisting this temptation will help prevent gossip and foster in us an inner quiet, staying centered on God and being more efficient in caring for our responsibilities. Those who fail to practice this bit of wisdom contribute to an "untranquil atmosphere of in-groups versus out-groups, [i]nvasion of privacy, meddling, envious comparison, backbiting, and other signs of communal turmoil [that] spoil family, professional, and religious life."[11]

Disciplining our heart and mind, and especially our tongue, is necessary if we are to avoid these imperfections and sins, keep an inner peace, and grow in the friendship and love we say we want with God. "If we can grow gradually in the attitude of returning to God in peaceful resignation when turmoil abounds [or when surrounded by grave injustice or violence to come to him hanging on the cross], we shall establish inner tranquility"[12] and be able to do what is just with the authority and strength of Jesus (Luke 4:31–36, especially v.36). The center where I live with God will be the storehouse of all the Spirit's wisdom and energy needed to live well my day, to

---

10. John of the Cross, "Counsels," 662–65.

11. Muto, *Words of Wisdom*, 65.

12. Muto, *Words of Wisdom*, 65.

do my part in the mission of Jesus, and to be the kind of person with whom others would enjoy sharing community.

SECOND COUNSEL: UNDERGO PATIENTLY THE IMPERFECTIONS OF OTHERS

John stresses how great growth takes place in our life with God if we strive to be more other-centered. How many of us dream of the ideal marriage, family, the perfect religious community or parish, or work setting, etc.? We all carry within us utopian hopes at some time or other, especially when we are young. The reality of living and working closely with others tempers this idealism. We become disappointed, irritated, and disillusioned by the various rough edges of others. Such disappointments can tempt us to complain about our bad luck and retreat into a private world, or we can meet the challenge and embrace the realities of relationships.

These encounters can bring us closer to God as we face the reality of a meddling in-law; a son or daughter who has poor boundaries; a micromanaging work colleague; or a hypercritical neighbor. We can respond out of love for God, or by uniting ourselves in silence with the suffering body of Christ, aware that some members of his body are in much more difficult situations than we are. "[We] are like the stone that must be chiseled and fashioned before being set in the building."[13] "Nothing chisels and fashions us quite as much as close contact with other people who seem to specialize in grinding away at our grandiosity."[14]

How do we handle those who point out our own shortcomings, provoke impatience and anger, make us feel incompetent, or leave us feeling taken for granted? We can either strike back with negative judgments and criticism and continue the cycle of mutual hurt and division; or, out of gratitude to, and *in imitation of,* Christ, we can bear it patiently and calmly. In this way we can "find inner quietude and joy in the Holy Spirit."[15]

Life is a school for learning how to love. It demands steady doses of reality for us to learn Christian love. Experiencing the rough edges in others and discovering the same in ourselves make for a perfect laboratory for purification and being honed in Christ. With God as our center, we learn to love, we grow emotionally, and we experience deeper knowledge and love for Christ.

13. Muto, *Words of Wisdom,* 20.

14. Muto, *Words of Wisdom,* 67.

15. Muto, *Words of Wisdom,* 20.

THIRD COUNSEL: PRACTICE VIRTUE, LIVE FOR GOD ALONE

We need to develop the habit of "seeking the one thing necessary" (see Luke 10:42); that is, to desire deeper union with Jesus and the Father; to seek in the spirit of the widow who gave her last two coins (Luke 21:1–4), to give our whole self to God. God must become deeply treasured by us to live this way habitually, especially in times that demand significant sacrifice. We soon find out what our motives are when we need to help others in a way that is difficult and not according to our preferences.

As a way of growing in this attitude, John of the Cross recommends our preferring to do what is "not the easy way out but the difficult pursuit of excellence, not the 'soft sell' but the rugged way of long hours and strict dedication, not a penchant for the pleasant or for what pays now, but a willingness to work hard to make something right, even if the labor demanded is distasteful."[16]

For example, I choose to set aside my feelings of hurt and anger at someone who accuses me wrongly (unless the accusations would destroy my reputation, and perhaps that of the group I belong to, for doing any good, of being considered trustworthy for any ministry/service.) I choose, instead, to turn the other cheek and unite myself with Christ as an opportunity to share in his passion.

Or again, I am quite bothered by things I cannot change, such as the personality of another. Instead of complaining and evoking the pity of others, I choose to be silent and give it all to Christ. Again, I unite myself with him, aware of my own imperfections and God's patience with me.

Or, still again, imagine yourself being a rather extroverted person and tending to take over in groups. You monitor this characteristic in yourself and choose to listen more. Or imagine just the opposite; you are quite introverted and dread debating with or relating to assertive people. Your choice of union with Christ can be to contribute what you know in situations like this, even at the risk of appearing not that knowledgeable on the topic or as intelligent as others in the group.

This third counsel, living for God alone, makes no sense unless Christ Jesus means everything to us. Crosses become much lighter when God is the North Star of our soul. This powerful love frees us from being slaves to our surface desires. Rather, it leads us, whether in times of abundance or

---

16. Muto, *Words of Wisdom*, 71.

want, in good times or bad, to be free in the Holy Spirit for the one great love of our life: Christ Jesus, our Savior.

FOURTH COUNSEL: SEEK SOLITUDE
AND SINGLE-HEARTED LIVING

The spiritually healthy person is one who has a balanced lifestyle. It is difficult to live this way when the secular culture rewards compulsive imbalance. The challenge is for us to be engaged in whatever is our responsibility without being so involved that we forget God. We can mindlessly live a harried life: cutting corners, not giving due attention to the people who deserve our presence and care. What protects against this spirit is our practicing an attentiveness to God's abiding presence in everything we do. We center ourselves in him and let go of our ego-centered needs. This counsel, then, is about healthy detachment in everything we do, keeping a mature spiritual perspective, seeking not our own pleasure but only God's honor and glory.

In all these counsels of John of the Cross, the determining factor is how much God means to us. In other words, to have a strong sense of detachment regarding persons and things, we need to be attached to God as the deepest love of our life. This happens when we spend regular quality time with God in prayer and in those spontaneous, informal times when we are alone and can go inside to be with him at our deepest center. Preferring to drive with the radio off, taking the opportunity to be with God while waiting in a doctor's office, or riding a train or airplane, can be moments for enjoying this best of friendships.

John offers these counsels to help us grow spiritually, emotionally, and psychologically as well, and to mature in the ways we live. This will greatly help us to grow in the dispositions necessary for contemplating: of being able to wait, to receive, and enjoy being present to God.

BUT GOD IS NOT DONE

One might think that a very conscientious application of self to these guidelines, plus working very hard to change one's behaviors that are expressions of the seven capital sins, will assure major reform for entering the latter dwelling places. The humbling truth is that while our efforts are most necessary and do bear significant fruit, they are the lesser factor in our transformation in Christ. We must work directly on rectifying our behaviors and, to the degree possible, our attitudes and values. This is the active part of a much more involved process than what first seems to be the case. Much more important than our efforts is the action of God bringing to our consciousness anything not in harmony with him and the relationship we have with him.

I refer particularly to the attitudes and values that are largely unconscious and cannot be accessed by us or changed without God's direct intervention. This phase of the process John of the Cross calls the passive night of the senses, which complements what we just reviewed (i.e., the active night of the senses). The passive night of the senses is what much of our next chapter addresses.

QUESTIONS FOR DISCUSSION AND FAITH-SHARING

- Of all the various disciplines presented above for our dying to self and responding to Christ's call to deeper availability and giving our entire self to him, which one is the most helpful for you, or the most challenging?

- When you think about St. Paul's description of our inner core as "the new man" or "hidden self," with "our life hidden with Christ in God," how do you respond—with what feelings, thoughts, especially desires? Have your times in prayer ever focused on this truth, this awesome mystery of who we really are in our depths? If not, does it inspire you to let it guide you as to what to pray on, to ask for? Do you see the realization of this mystery implied in your deepest desires and longings, in what you pray for yourself, for others, and for the world?

7

The Passive Dark Night
A Radical Purging

NEEDING GOD TO INTERVENE

NED IS A HAPPILY married man who anticipates ten more years of work before retirement. Recently, he became a grandfather for the fifth time. His relationship with God is all-important to him, and he feels a great desire for a deeper life with God. He is determined, with the help of the Lord, to face in himself new awarenesses of pride and other self-centered traits. To dispose himself to God's purifying activity, he reads good spiritual books, consults at times a trained spiritual guide, prays daily for at least thirty minutes, and makes an annual weekend contemplative retreat. He especially enjoys praying with others in biweekly, silent meditation sessions.

Over the last few years, Ned has been experiencing intense longings for God; sometimes it seems God pursues him, more than he pursues God. His prayer has evolved into what Teresa of Avila calls the prayer of active recollection and at times the prayer of quiet. Occasionally, he experiences brief moments of sweet union. Ned's way is to focus on the wound in Jesus' side (John 19:37; 20:27–28) and God in the depths of Jesus (1 Cor 2:10 and Eph 3:18–20). His prayer is wordless, except perhaps using a mantra to steady his focus—with no specific thoughts, memories, or future planning; just being present, loving quietly, and resting in the Heart of Jesus. Some days are very full, others dry and distracted. But overall, his prayer is marked by an abiding longing for God. During his day, Ned experiences these longings welling up within. It is so touching to realize that God is initiating his prayer. At times he feels he can never get enough of being with God, gazing at and entering the Heart of Jesus, pierced for him and the entire world. He is struck with wonder and at times wells up with tears. It is all so beautiful, something he knows he does not deserve. He is very humbled by it all. What a gift!

What embarrasses Ned is the contrast between these amazing blessings and his sense of being so imperfect because of his numerous faults and self-focused habits. The closer he comes to God, the stronger his sense of how meagre his love is, how extensive his ego and sinfulness! His trust in God has freed him to be more honest and truthful about his actions and attitudes. Divine Love has sensitized him in remarkable ways and gently urges him to conversion. Some of his tears are precisely because of this awareness. Love's wound is opening him: to a much greater appreciation of his need for a Savior; to God's unconditional acceptance of him as he is now; and finally, to a wonderfully consoling sense of God's tender mercies toward him. He has never experienced love this personal, generous, pure, and reverent. Like the apostle Thomas, Ned exclaims at times, "My Lord and my God!" (John 20:28). Sometimes there comes up inside a painful ache to love God back with everything in himself and then infinitely more. He wonders: Will there ever be a day when he can love God as God deserves to be loved? It would be an unbearable pain if there were no realizing this longing! He keenly feels the enormous limits of his own efforts to realize these deeper desires.

Like Ned, when we have entered the fourth dwelling places and beyond, we feel a certain powerlessness about progressing much further through our own efforts. We experience core habits, often rooted in family-of-origin issues. This state of soul will require something more than what we have been doing so far. God must become more directly involved, through a process which John of the Cross calls the passive night of the senses and spirit. This process engages much of what are self-focused habits often entrenched in our unconscious. God alone can disentangle and purge them. Our part is to let go and let God do what only God can do.

HOW GOD INTERVENES

What triggers this state of soul? Sometimes it is God who directly provokes it. For example, in prayer that leaves us feeling quite dry over a long time and tempted to quit. Often it comes through the relentless demands of life itself or from taking on too many commitments. Sometimes it comes through a frightful burnout experience in our work or through a serious, prolonged sickness. Then there can be certain people around us who impact us negatively or irritate or contradict us often, and through them God does his deeper work of purifying and recreating us.

Such experiences can evoke a humbling awareness of how we are not as holy or virtuous as we first thought.[1] We notice how partial and discriminating we can be about those to whom we give our time and attention; also how judgmental, even prejudicial we can be about certain others; how we insist on our perspective being right; how we fantasize about being praised for our successes; or how we feel superior to others. We can also be left feeling overwhelmed, defeated, afraid/anxious about losing God and our way with God; or more intensely: feeling powerless, abandoned, alone, confused, even hopeless. Then there are those harrowing moments of experiencing the limits of our body after an injury, major surgery, or simply aging and becoming dependent on others for assistance. Might this be something of what Jesus warned Peter, the apostle, about when he would grow old (John 21:18)?

We can also be taken into this passive dark night through experiences, like being misunderstood, harshly judged, and rejected; failing to find anyone who understands the troubles of our soul; greatly fearing a nervous, psychological breakdown; or being terminally ill, or of dying and dreading what follows death. Flashbacks of great abuse and memories of being humiliated and making big mistakes, followed by rage and self-criticism, can set us up for this intense state of purgation. So, too, enduring great financial loss, or loss of job, reputation, or health, or no longer being trusted or respected. Other traumatic events can trigger this painful process, like a lifeless marriage, including the humiliation of the other's infidelity and then undergoing divorce; betrayal by someone we trusted or idealized; the death, or especially the suicide, of our child, parent, or close friend. These kinds of devastating events can leave us feeling abandoned by God.

Many grandparents feel something of this passive night when grieving about their adult children not raising their children as Christians, perceiving that they do not value Jesus enough to want their offspring to know and love him. With it can come recriminating thoughts: "What did I do wrong? What should I have done or not done to have avoided such a loss of faith?"

---

1. See Niere, *Gospel of Contemplation*, 28–29.

Sometimes these experiences can open us up to a shattering experience of how we have misunderstood and imaged God, leaving us disillusioned and angry with him, and leading even to a crisis of faith. Persistent, painful memories and fears can fill us with dread and loathing for our self and certain others, even to the point of murderous and suicidal thoughts accompanied by psychosomatic problems.

Note that these foundation-shaking experiences can affect us physically, psychologically, and/or spiritually. A medical doctor might be needed to help us with the physical symptoms, a psychologist with the mental challenges we face, and a knowledgeable spiritual guide/prayerful person who understands these chapters of the disciplining and purification of our soul and can recognize the hand of God in it all. It is possible we could need help at all three levels simultaneously!

Experiences like these can last a long time—for months or even years—or they can take place in short, intense periods. They can be mild or strong enough to overwhelm us. They will reflect the degree of freedom from imperfection/sin and degree of love to which God wills to raise us. They can be mild in their impact or strong enough to overwhelm us.

EXAMPLES FROM HISTORY AND SCRIPTURE

Do many or only a few suffer the more intense versions of these purifying experiences? Only God knows. Yet we have witnessed in the last few centuries, as well as our present one, so many, *many* people suffering beyond what most of us can imagine. For example, what the native peoples of North America and Mexico have suffered at the hands of some European immigrant-settlers. Then in the USA and South America, Africans who suffered enslavement, the splitting up of their families, and especially the emasculation of their adult males. Then the Jewish Holocaust as well as the genocides in western China, the Congo, Cambodia, Bosnia-Herzegovina, Rwanda, and Syria/Iraq. Also, there are the horrendous wounds from sexual violations visited upon young and old, some by people of helping professions both religious and secular. Then, too, in the brothels of the world, and in the trafficking of children and young adults. The lifelong effects of these unspeakable sufferings, especially the struggle to trust others or believe in their own self-worth, make them instances of Christ crucified. Most, it seems, are unaware of the mystery of Christ's death and resurrection they carry within themselves.

We can find many other examples of these trials in the Hebrew Scriptures: the lives of Abraham, Moses, Ruth, Esther, David, and Hosea to name a few; in the New Testament in Jesus especially when agonizing in the garden of Gethsemane and while hanging on the cross; in Mother Mary and Mary Magdalene while at Calvary; in Sts. Peter and Paul and members of the early church expelled from the synagogue and blamed for the disastrous intervention of the Roman army. All the apostles and close followers of Jesus during the weekend of Jesus' death and even in the first moments of encountering the risen Christ: they experienced something of this mysterious dark night while being transformed in Christ.

I have recognized something of these harrowing experiences of deep purification in the biography of St. Oscar Romero, a prophet in his own time pleading for justice for the simple farmers of his land, El Salvador, and then being assassinated in 1980 while praying Mass.[2] Another in the riveting account of Fr. Walter Ciszek, a Jesuit who, while being held in Russia as a suspected spy, survived the hatred and intense persecution of the Russian communists from 1939 till 1963.[3] So, too, the French monks at the Trappist monastery in Tibhirine, Algeria, in the early to mid-1990s, struggled with many fears in the face of death threats to leave Algeria. They decided after much prayer and communal discernment to stay, even though they knew it meant certain death. Like Jesus, who could not run from the garden of Gethsemane and be true to himself, they stood their ground as witnesses to their everlasting commitment to God. In May 1996, seven of these nine monks sacrificed their lives, being kidnapped and executed. God alone knows the sufferings they experienced while waiting for the final blow.[4]

The book of Job and the gripping story of the prophet Jeremiah, especially verses 3:1–20 of Lamentations, describe in detail the intense sufferings some people can undergo during this purifying process. St. Teresa of Avila endured untold doubts, troubles, and especially abuses of authority by some bishops and priests during her efforts to implement renewal of her communities of women Carmelites. John of the Cross also suffered unmentionable horrors and hate-filled punishment at the hands of fellow Carmelites who vigorously resisted his initiatives for reform. St. Ignatius of Loyola and St. Francis of Assisi had their own painful moments while establishing their religious orders.

2. See Brockman, *Romero*.

3. See Ciszek and Flaherty, *He Leadeth Me*, ch. 7.

4. Plank, "When an A-Dieu Takes on a Face.

Abraham Lincoln, likewise, while guiding the US during the American Civil War, suffered serious threats of assassination at the beginning of both his first and second terms as president. During the war, he experienced many frustrations with military leaders he depended on but who in the end failed him. He also struggled greatly with how far he could advance the cause of freeing the slaves without the union of the states coming apart. In his personal life he suffered the tragic death of one of his children. Then there were the scandalous spending sprees his wife would go on, her mental breakdown, and the public ways she greatly embarrassed him.[5] Lincoln's faith in God was truly remarkable during his lonely, personal dark night and the nation's dark night. He became something of an image of Christ, the savior, especially in the way he was hated and assassinated by those who resented his freeing the slaves and the economic and social changes this brought about for the nation.

We all get our turn in experiencing something of this purification if we are serious about following Jesus. It forces us to decide whether to embrace our situation and grow from it or adopt strategies for avoiding this passive dark night experience.

WAYS OF AVOIDING THE DARK NIGHT

John of the Cross mentions three common ways[6] for us to avoid or alleviate the stress and pain of what he calls the trials and storms of the soul when going through the dark night. First, we may gravitate toward immediate sensual pleasure (e.g., overeating, drinking to excess, indulging in heightened eroticism and craving sexual pleasure, entertainment, and trivial diversions). Second, we can get angry at little things as well as major ones; being impatient, moody, blaming others, publicly complaining about this and that to others or to God; obsessing over thoughts of self-pity, feelings of being treated unfairly by God; fixating on trying to prove our innocence. Third, we can experience heightened anxiety about what the future holds, about losing control and predictability in life, or in having exaggerated fears about our health or dangers to our safety or to the whole world. This state of soul can include much confusion about God and our faith life. It could involve scruples.

5. See Trueblood, *Abraham Lincoln*.

6. See Coombs and Nemeck, *Way of Spiritual Direction*, 85, for a clear and contemporary wording of the wisdom of John of the Cross.

THE DARK NIGHT: ITS MEANING

Why is this purgative, cleansing, healing, and transforming dynamic of our life called a dark night? Why dark? Why a night?

First,

> 'dark' is an analogy for painful . . . [it] accentuates all the forms of adversity [like many cited above] which we can undergo in the course of living and being transformed . . . [they come from inside us]: our own inner poverty . . . emotional weaknesses, psychological limitations, personal sinfulness, addictions, codependency, attachments . . . [also] from the outside: disease, harsh words, unjust accusations, etc. God integrates all these pains into our night . . . to convert [them] into good . . .[7]

The process is a night because it is "symbolic of the mysterious activity of God within us and all around us . . . [It is] also during the night that the Lord probes our heart and examines our inmost being . . . and displays knowledge of him[self]."[8]

John of the Cross says this process is a night[9] because it will take us beyond our attractions to possessions, material things, and pleasures, beyond the securities we seek from the glitter of the world of senses. It moves us from living mostly at the first two levels of Diagram 1 to the deeper ones.

Further, it is dark, he says, because when we enter what Teresa calls the fourth dwelling places we experience God and the things of God as more attractive. Being weaned from our attachments to material things is like being deprived of light by which objects can be seen. For our senses, it is a darkness.

Also, this invasion of God into our soul coaxes us increasingly beyond trusting in our own reasoning and accomplishments, beyond what we are able to control through our memory, imagination, intellect, and will. In so loving us, God encourages us to allow him to lead us to a new kind of knowing, to walk by the light of a greater faith in him. If we consent, we will experience God's world, thanks to an awakening of delicate, marvelous sensitivities in our soul, which I will address later.

Lastly, John says this process is experienced as a night because God is a dark night to human beings in this life. God is infinitely beyond what

---

7. See Coombs and Nemeck, *O Blessed Night*, 70–71.

8. Coombs and Nemeck, *O Blessed Night*, 71.

9. Coombs and Nemeck, *O Blessed Night*, 77.

our very limited mind, memory, and imagination can grasp. He is beyond all names and images. There is much more we do not know about God than we do know. His revelation is the only light by which we can journey home to him.

FUTURE NEEDS FOR NED

Let us return to Ned and his spiritual journey. Suppose he becomes more aware of his impatience with certain work associates, especially with those of less seniority. He admits to an undue desire for praise and public recognition, especially with authority figures. For awhile he has been aware of these self-centering faults. Now they have become "thorns in his side" (2 Cor 12:7–10), humbling reminders of his need for God to do what he cannot seem to grow beyond.

In the passive night of his senses, Ned is being confronted with what is contrary to God, certain impurities in his soul, manifest in pride-filled judgments, critical gossiping, and in exaggerating his successes in hopes of being given a salary raise. In moments like this, Ned feels petty, more sinful and unlike God than ever. It is God's loving light that is bringing to the surface this embarrassing self-knowledge, like a spotlight on what has been hidden. God, then, is to blame! Yet not really, because any pain Ned suffers in this struggle is not directly caused by God but is the result of Ned's resistance to having to own this part of himself. He must face it and bring it to God for healing, or at least for acceptance if it is not God's will to heal it now. This must be the choice of anyone wanting to pass through the narrow gate and desiring to grow into the latter dwelling places. Ned's deepening trust of God makes it possible for God to effect the miracle of his transformation in Christ.

Until there is a deep trust in God, and unless we bring our whole soul to him (Jer 29:13), these dark night experiences will overwhelm us. It is imperative that we unite our sufferings with those of the crucified Jesus and, perhaps, weep with him through the pain, the chaos we are enduring. We must hope against hope that God is bringing about something awesomely beautiful in us, more than we could ever ask for or imagine (Eph 3:20).

SUMMARY STATEMENTS ABOUT THIS PROCESS

Coombs and Nemeck make some very helpful observations about this process: first, that the dark night is practical. It meets us exactly in the concrete aspects of where we are still not free. "The specific form that purification takes at any moment is tailored by God to all the particulars, no matter how seemingly trivial or insignificant, in each human journey."[10] Second, rather than our making this process happen, we undergo it. We are *receiving* salvation, an action by God; it is not something we do. "He breaks our shackles so that we can move freely out of our attachments . . . more deeply into him."[11] Third, the process always moves us forward, and through it we experience peace and joy because we taste new freedoms, even when we sense God is not done with us, that we need further purification.

If this process is to have its desired effects, then it is critically important that we learn to receive, to accept, to be patient, and to wait in prayer for God to work our transformation in and through this process of darkness. Often our prayer is precisely the suffering accepted as such. We choose to face the struggle with Jesus at our side. Our prayer can be significantly deepened by turning to Jesus in his passion (e.g., holding a crucifix in our lap and looking steadily with grateful love at him, or imagining ourselves kneeling with him at the rock in Gethsemane and sharing with him our fears, humiliations, and loneliness). Doing this can open us up to a profound communion with him and give us remarkable strength to bear our share of the cross.

We can also find strength by paying attention to the sufferings of other people, of Christ's body today, focusing, for example, on what so many refugees or immigrants endure. Likewise, focusing on what cancer patients, victims of abuse, and the incarcerated suffer can greatly help in removing focus from ourselves and opening us up to profound communion with the Crucified Jesus. Carrying these people in our heart and their wounds as the wounds of Christ crucified will expand enormously our knowledge of and love for God.

10. Coombs and Nemeck, *O Blessed Night*, 75.
11. Coombs and Nemeck, *O Blessed Night*, 76.

ABUNDANT BLESSINGS AND HEALINGS

This process of deep purification is truly a liberation from the fleshpots of our Egypt, from much of the hold that the seven capital sins have on us, especially our pride and little vanities, greed, and resentments. It has led us through the desert, leaving us feeling perhaps like the wandering Hebrews journeying toward the promised land. The change in our soul is cause for much joy and gratitude. We experience an increase of faith, hope, and charity as important gifts in this transformational process. We appreciate now more than ever how true it is that without God we can do absolutely nothing, and that our motivation is so often mixed; that we are powerless to do anything good by ourselves. We now appreciate, better than ever, how we need guidance and that it is vitally necessary for us to assume a humble, listening stance toward God if we are going to stay on the narrow road and realize what Jesus promises. As Teresa of Avila insists, if we are to grow beyond the early stages of the spiritual journey, we must be open to learn who we really are and how much we need God to gain significant self-knowledge.

This priceless gift of new freedom, thanks to God's goodness, is accomplished not only in our receiving a great increase in the gifts of faith, hope, and charity, but also in noticeable growth in the Beatitudes, especially in being more poor in spirit. Further, our prayer has developed from discursive meditation, with its use of images, to the prayer of quiet (i.e., wordless acceptance and surrender, a stance of loving attentiveness and receptivity). We feel more peaceful, more grounded and expanded in our soul, and more connected with others.

At the heart of this awesome change is our becoming much more who we truly are and being able to accept our personal history, unresolved problems, and inclinations to self-centering which still live in us. At the same time, we experience God's amazing personal love for us and promise that in his time and way, we will be taken beyond all that is still unresolved and be completely transformed in Christ. All subsequent healings emerge from this foundational conversion.

The self, now hidden with Christ in God (Col 3:3), experiences now a greater freedom to accept others as they are. We can live more peacefully, even in the midst of differences, imperfections, and conflicts, and with much greater hope in God. We are able to love more like we have been loved by Christ. We are now living the life of the risen Christ (Gal 2:19b–20) and experiencing a Godly wisdom (1 Cor 2:5–13) and patience in our daily living. The connection between our spirit and the Spirit of God is noticeably stronger when we are doing what we are called to say or do. All our relationships with other individuals, with family, church, and other institutions, even with the wider world, can get healed when this foundational relationship, our self with our self, is healed.

We experience this Gracious Mystery of God, the deeply satisfying water Jesus refers to in John 7:37–38, welling up inside us. These brief visitations of God are surprising, very beautiful, and often quite powerful. We know they are real, that they are of God, and that we are not inventing them, because they are so strong, enough to overpower us and lift us beyond all our limits. This depth of love evokes very powerful desires to reciprocate love beyond anything we imagined possible. We find ourselves saying something like:

> I have found a love that sometimes captures me, at times even ravishes me and has led me to reevaluate everything in light of him (Phil 3:7–11). I have never met anyone like him; nothing comes even close to him. I have come to see all things in him who loved me and gave himself up for me. I so want to love him back in the same way, like the widow who gave her last two coins, or the merchant who sold everything so that he could have that one precious pearl. Christ Jesus is that pearl, the only person worth giving my all for. I want to live for him and die for him.

The joy and freedom of living in the fourth and more advanced dwelling places eventually become habitual. It is in the fourth set that the spiritual Copernican revolution described earlier begins to be our normal way of living and praying; the narrow road becomes the only choice that makes any sense for living our life. In the next chapter, we will look more closely at the quality of life and special challenges experienced in the fourth dwelling places.

QUESTIONS FOR DISCUSSION AND FAITH-SHARING

- In what ways have you experienced something of this dark night process in which you suffered a loss or went through a difficult situation with someone?

- Name some of the graces that have come your way thanks to your undergoing/suffering through a period of the dark night.

- What saints or biblical characters do you revere greatly for their dark-night sufferings and subsequent fidelity to God? Name a contemporary of yours whom you know, or know about, who lived or still lives something of this mystery of transformative suffering and spiritual growth. Describe the circumstances of their situation.

SECTION III

Spiritually Maturing

8

The Fourth Dwelling Places

IN THE PREVIOUS CHAPTER, I provided a short profile of Ned, a man who was living in the fourth dwelling places. Most of that chapter focused on the kinds of purification Ned and others in the fourth dwelling places can encounter. These dwelling places, however, demand additional explanation, which now follows.

The fourth dwelling places mark the beginning of a new, more authentic Christian way of living. Being moved now by God's love to trust him more and be opened to new ways of action in our prayer and daily lives, we are freer to admit to our ways of being controlling, judgmental, and feeling self-righteous. "[Our] idols [have been] not just personal loves and possessions, but especially idols of power, prestige, [safety and security], control and dominance [that encourage a life of self-absorption and] neglect in our immediate relationships . . . [also] blindness to the poor and their situation in our world and other issues of justice in society."[1] In these fourth dwelling places we are being invited to surrender to a loving, trustworthy God; a God who has been waiting for us to say: "Yes, I will trust you; I am ready to make the journey with you to freedom, whatever the cost." We learn that our limits and vulnerability are not something to fear or be ashamed of or avoid but are our biggest assets for growing into the freedom of Christ. We

---

1. O'Sullivan, *Pilgrimage to God*, 10.

experience the paradoxical truth: in our human weaknesses there is available a divine strength that empowers, consoles, and reassures us.

God has chosen the poverty of our human condition, embraced fully in Jesus Christ, to be the very means through which he saves us. When we pay close attention to the world's stories of suffering, failure, betrayals, and dying, we might be more alert to how these human limitations and our mortality are the locus of God's saving actions. It seems no one in their right mind would invent a religion that proclaims a God who saves his creatures this way. We would insist that God show his power in a victorious manner, be more efficient, more reasonable, and even impressive. Yet the poverty of our human condition is God's Way! The cost might seem to be too much, too counterintuitive, too scary. It seems to be the principle reason why many choose to stay in the third dwelling places, in the Egypt largely of their own making, and live a culturally compromised version of the Gospel.

God, however, keeps coaxing us in prayer and through good people to come closer, to go deeper. By his evoking strong desires for intimacy and a mutual sharing of love, we eventually lose our fears and find the courage to say yes to his offer of deep friendship and love. The joy that wells up from within, the new possibilities for life and relationship, seem boundless. God sustains us through the inevitable trials and sacrifices till we are blessed with a stabilized, continuous awareness of God's presence and love in our daily life and relationships.

The welling up of this Gracious Mystery or underground River of Divine Life provides a vivid and felt sense of the mystery that God is working in us while we live in the fourth and later dwelling places. Teresa of Avila speaks of this experience in terms of two words, *contentos* and *gustos,* to contrast our former ways of praying to a new way of praying (and living also).

CONSOLATIONS AND DEEPER DELIGHTS

Teresa describes *contentos* (consolations) as "the experiences we ourselves acquire through our own meditation and petitions to the Lord, those that proceed from our own nature . . . [they] arise from the virtuous work itself that we perform, and it seems that we have earned them through our own efforts and are rightly consoled for having engaged in such deeds."[2] Often these emotional moments are accompanied by inspirational insights which

2. *IC,* IV, 1, 4.

help us on our journey to God. Such consolations emerge from the level of the senses.

Gustos, translated as spiritual delights, are quite different. They proceed directly from God, welling up unexpectedly into our awareness from the underground River of Divine Life.

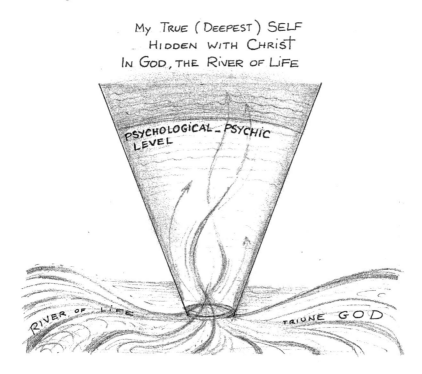

Diagram 3: Our True Self Hidden in Christ

Teresa says they leave us absorbed in and awed by what our mind sees. *Gustos* significantly open our consciousness to God's love and mercy, as well as encourage our receptivity to God's actions. With these blessings come feelings of unworthiness and deep gratitude, but especially a keener awareness of how unlike God we are. Particularly, we become more aware of smug, self-righteous attitudes like: "I can take care of myself" and "I am a rather virtuous person; look at all the good I do. I am not one of those big sinners." We see more clearly why we need a Savior.

The more important change, however, comes in the way we pray. The way we relate to God significantly affects the way we live. Part of learning to let go and surrender to God, then, is to let God lead in our prayer and pray in us. As was explained to some extent in chapter 5, we are stirred to love more, to let go of all thinking and *just be* with God. We are meeting God as infinitely good and lovable while we gaze on him with great love, not on an image of him, but *on him*, with increasingly strong desires for union and total self-giving. We learn not to seek a specific experience of God (God is *not* an experience, *not* a feeling or insight) but rather to receive, to let God be *however God wants to be* with us and simply rest there with God. To become accustomed to a kind of prayer without the aid of concepts, images, or the usual consolations that come from discursive meditation reflects significant maturation in our relationship with God. God blesses us with a more adultlike faith and stronger trust; we become increasingly at home with steadily gazing on God as our preferred way of praying, even when God is vaguely perceived. We grow to not think much but to simply love much, as Teresa of Avila describes this prayer.[3] The great blessing is that "God [is purifying] our too narrow understanding both of God and of the self as [he] draws [us] into inner stillness.[4]

PRAYER IMPACTS LIFE

Consider the impact this new, more surrendered way of praying can have on our daily life. Imagine how it can improve our ways of listening and engaging in conversation, the ways we live in community.[5] Ponder how it can more likely inspire us to act with daring, even with prophetic zeal, to go beyond our usual comfort zones of economic, social, and racial similarities. We will be more open to involving ourselves in care for those who struggle, lack the necessities of life, and are rejected and feared. It can inspire us to take on more of God's dream, his cares shown in Jesus' priorities, and bring us into a more meaningful, happier, fulfilling life. We will desire more intensely to proclaim this unforgettable love capturing our heart (Isa 40:9–11).

3. *IC,* IV, 1, 7.

4. Seelaus, *Distractions in Prayer,* 37.

5. See the writings of Marshall Rosenberg on learning what he calls nonviolent ways of communicating for enjoying deeper interpersonal communication. His method cultivates patience in listening well to the other, focusing on what the other truly needs and values, and asking questions of the other until clarity about the other's needs and core values emerge. This approach fosters mutual recognition of deep emotional and spiritual needs and, in turn, encourages discipline of our ego: respect, compassion, and peaceful resolution between the persons or groups involved.

We also become freer in accepting others, less judgmental and critical, and allow them to be themselves. Oh, how this would make parenting children and teens much easier! We trust God's direction and providence for others, without having to replace God by taking too much responsibility for their lives and salvation. While God brings about spiritual growth in God's way, whether in few or many years, we lovingly encourage and support one another on this journey. Blessed with this new freedom, we can see other people more the way God sees them. We are becoming wonderful examples of the spiritual Copernican revolution.

A NEW WAY OF PRAYING

More needs to be said about the prayer of gazing steadily on God. While it seems that nothing is going on in this way of praying, something profoundly beautiful is being given in our depths. At first our intellect or understanding has a difficult adjustment to make since it roams about, seeking according to its past habits to cling to familiar concepts and images of God. Gradually, we learn to hold our attention, calmly and lovingly, on God alone.[6] During this transition we sometimes experience dryness because our senses are not being engaged. Further, our mind and imagination cannot cope with this "inflow of God,"[7] as John of the Cross calls this mysterious action. God's way of being present is beyond and deeper than our intellect, imagination, and emotions. In time we learn to intuitively accept and trust this silent, loving Divine Presence "invading" and moving in us (John 14:23). We learn to be still, quiet in body and mind, while being present and lovingly attentive to God. Teresa calls this the prayer of quiet.

Sometimes the movement in this delicate way of prayer may include a sweet touch of God's presence, or an intimation of his immensity, or a sense of his boundless love and joy. These spiritual delights (*gustos*) can come during formal prayer time but also in our daily activities. All is surprise, all is gift. We cannot control these delights but only dispose ourselves to God and let him bless us with them however and whenever he wishes. However, what is more important than any consolation or delight (*contentos* or *gustos*) of God is the gift of God himself, and that is what the contemplative learns to be open to, without condition, rather than seek any specific blessing.

---

6. See Green's *When the Well Runs Dry*, ch. 6, for likening the experience of contemplative prayer to that of a swimmer floating on water.

7. John of the Cross, *Dark Night*, ch. 5, sec. 1.

THE INTERIOR SENSES OF OUR SOUL

One fascinating dimension of the prayer of quiet that opens us to our deepest desires is called *the interior senses* of our soul. Teresa does not address this feature of contemplative prayer but certainly implies it in the way she describes its traits. What are these interior senses? They are intuitive, graced sensitivities of our soul, analogous to the five senses of our body. We can speak of experiencing intimately the presence of God, for example, in terms of what St. Ignatius of Loyola calls "smelling the infinite fragrance and tasting the sweetness of the Divinity . . . (or) touch(ing and) embrac(ing and) kiss(ing) the places where such persons put their feet and sit."[8] The great Franciscan theologian, St. Bonaventure (d. 1274), expounds extensively on these capacities of our soul in his *The Soul's Journey into God;*[9] while St. Ignatius of Loyola (d. 1556) in his *Spiritual Exercises* directs the retreatant to employ these inner senses during the final, usually fourth, repetition of prayer on a particular Gospel scene. By the last period, Ignatius would have us focus on just one aspect of the scene that consoles us greatly. Then moving beyond any image, we would rest in the quiet, in deep communion with the One who drew us.[10] We might give ourselves to God in an intimate embrace of spirit to Spirit, or through a touch of the Divine depths. In that state of soul, we are open to any of the delights (*gustos*) God might wish to give in the prayer of quiet. Eventually this kind of wordless quiet becomes our usual and preferred way of praying. We will have outgrown imaginative prayer as our usual way and feel drawn with much love to be centered in God, abiding there in his presence and goodness.

I have guided many retreatants who begin in imaginative prayer, focused on a Gospel scene, and after three or four one-hour-long repetitions, they move with increasing simplicity to focus on one aspect and stay there for quite some time with wordless, loving attention. For example, while holding the infant Christ they might press very gently the child's heart to their own and remain there; or, as one woman retreatant did, she chose to nurse the infant Christ, so natural did it seem to her. Others spent their time holding their hand on the nailed feet of Jesus crucified. Those who pray in this way can be present to Christ as an infant or as an adult, crucified or risen, and, moving beyond the image, encounter him in the now with

8. Fleming, *Draw Me into Your Friendship*, paras.124 & 125.

9. See *The Soul's Journey into God In Bonaventure.*

10. Fleming, *Draw Me into Your Friendship*, para. 124.

profound intimacy. They are refreshed by God, probably with *contentos* but much more with *gustos* if God so wills, through the mediating power of these interior spiritual sensitivities. They are experiencing the beginnings of contemplative prayer.

EFFECTS OF SUCH INTIMATE KNOWING

Blessings, especially intimate knowledge and anointings like these, soon draw us away from the attachments and self-righteous thinking that are so typical of life in the third dwelling places. They evoke new desires and courage to live for God in ways characteristic of the fourth and later dwelling places. Soon we find in our heart the desire to give everything. We gain insight that this miracle emerging in us is the mirror image of Divine Love being consumed with love for us. He, the Savior, sells everything and lays down his life for us so that he might attract us into a deep friendship and experience a profound love for each other. His will is that someday each of us will be part of a great and eternal communion or family made up of those who love like he does, with all they have and are.

Thanks to our growing, intense love for God, we are graced to be habitually aware of the presence and goodness, the truth and beauty of God: in nature and the cosmos, in our friends and enemies, in the world in all its pains, sufferings, and death—in all kinds of experiences. We know we are not projecting our wishes but are knowing God as never before, with a delicacy of soul that is exquisite, even breathtaking at times. We are seeing with new depths. We are hearing the divine music in various experiences and noticing the joy and playfulness of God in creation. We are not inventing these experiences but recognizing them as what corresponds to our divinely given capacities. They stir our depths. They have a ring of unquestioned authenticity. They become more intensified in the later dwelling places and "impel us to leave behind the intellect and understanding and to rely only on desire, the fire of the Spirit within"[11] to bring us into the heart of God and the depths of joy for which we have been made. No wonder they leave us stammering to describe what has happened. Our prayer takes on, then, a more mystical, unmediated quality, effected by God's Spirit directly touching our spirit. We are held with awe by the purity of such a gift and appreciate deeply how such a beautiful encounter is a glimpse of heaven, a taste of the fullness for which we are longing.

11. Delio, *Crucified Love*, 65.

FUTURE CHALLENGES

In the meantime, whether on days of being distracted and dry, or on days of being very centered and steadily present to God, we are being given the strength to continue our journey with God down the narrow road to increasing self-knowledge and deepening humility and gratitude. St. Teresa says that to lose courage in this search for our transformation in Christ is, sadly, to backtrack. It will set us up for boredom, loneliness, and distress. Prayer then becomes perfunctory and dry because we are avoiding a key part of our true self: we are avoiding God waiting for us in the very issue or situation we need to face.

Our challenges, then, will not be problems to solve but points of entry for our encountering Gracious Mystery and the empowerment of God. We will need to face our challenges with a sense of trust that God is at our side; we will need to ask him to help us persevere and approach these challenges as opportunities for growth, to find him and our authentic self in them. We will need to be "determined with determination" to stay the course of this spiritual journey. There are no quick-and-easy formulae for resolving unhealed memories or wounded relationships, or for stepping into an uncertain future, try though we might. These are among the typical crosses that Divine Love might have us embrace, not to fear them or be embarrassed by them, but to trust him that he will be there to lift us up and guide us in whatever we must face. Hence the critical need for our being faithful in listening for and finding him through regular, personal prayer and helpful spiritual guidance.

PEOPLE IN THE FOURTH DWELLING PLACES

Let us suppose Fr. Newman, cited in chapter 3, is invited by a fellow priest friend to a retreat and that during the retreat Fr. Newman has a profound encounter with Jesus. What holds his attention and strikes him deeply is St. Paul's saying, "You know the grace of our Lord Jesus Christ, that though he was rich, *yet for your sake* he became poor, so that by his poverty *you* might become rich" (2 Cor 8:9). Fr. Newman had heard this verse numerous times before but now hears it as if for the first time. He is overwhelmed by its emphasis on Jesus' personal, sacrificial love for him. These words, sounding so powerfully in his spirit, stay with him during the rest of the retreat and for weeks afterwards, moving him many times to tears of sorrow, gratitude, and much praise. In the following weeks he recognizes with much embarrassment how self-centered and un-Christlike he has been over the years in seeking titles and clerical prestige, in favoring the parish's well-to-do members, and in being so controlling about the operations of the parish. He is saddened to notice how his love for the Lord has been lukewarm, even miserly compared to the Lord's love for him. He experiences a healthy shame about how he has lived some of his life so far as a priest. So humbled and deeply touched by the love of Jesus so abundantly poured out for him, Fr. Newman desires to love God in return with all he has and is. God's grace moves him to a Copernicanlike change in his values and life focus. These unforgettable experiences constitute a new sense of vocation for him to become a more authentic man and loving priest. Jesus is inviting him to be, more than ever before, his disciple and friend, and to live for God with all he has and is. Fr. Newman is finally, through this great grace, discovering his true self, a beautiful self, and experiencing the joy of giving this self to the One who has waited a long time for his coming home. Newman is experiencing God and his brother and Savior, Jesus, as the deepest love of his life.

What follows this profound encounter with Jesus and the Father, however, will be the day-to day demands of a new self-honesty regarding the ways he is still unconverted in some of his attitudes and values. Recurring distractions in his prayer will signal these areas. Dryness in prayer will reflect his unfamiliarity with God communicating himself as a silent inflow of the Spirit. Monthly meetings with a guide who understands the workings of personal prayer and the need for detachment will help immensely, as well as his praying at least thirty minutes each day.

More important than anything to his progress, however, will be the deeper desires God will unlock from his depths as time goes by. These should free him significantly to allow God to do in him whatever God wants, in God's way, and in God's time. The rest of his life, if he is willing and persevering, will be a journey toward total surrender to and greater reverence for God, while becoming increasingly awed by and secure in God's love for him.

Our journey into the latter dwelling places builds on these promising beginnings in the fourth dwelling places by letting God become our center, our first and last truth, our first and deepest love, and the initiator in each moment. Our soul will be blessed with intimations of God's boundless life by our entering his Heart and seeing people and the world from there. We will experience there something of his compassion for humanity's state of spiritual weakness and need for Christ Jesus. We will readily relate to this inspiring saying: "What does the Lord require of you but to do justice, and to love kindness, and to walk humbly with your God" (Mic 6:8). At the same time, we might find the face of God in someone we are serving and awaken to our need to let the Spirit take us deeper. Those we serve can sometimes be our teachers and channels of God's grace.

Hopefully, this will happen for Fr. Newman and he will eventually accept what John of the Cross calls the darkness of faith as his usual way of praying and living, also trusting more that God is working something wonderful in him. This blessing would manifest itself at times as a joy and peace that comes in prayer and at times during his priestly ministry. The resurrected Christ will move him as well with powerful desires to tell others—indeed, the whole world—this almost-too-good-to-believe Good News about who Jesus and the Father are (John 17:3). Newman's ministries will be so much more Christ-centered and reflect great gratitude and love. Alleluia!

At the same time, it is very important that those in the fourth dwelling places not settle there, as if this new knowledge and peace in God were the realization of all God has for them. There is so much more waiting to be given, and wise guidance is necessary to encourage us to seek God and deeper conversion while not confusing such with the peace and joy that can be found at times in this initial stage of contemplative prayer. These beautiful, interior gifts can become a subtle attachment, a sweetness to our spirit that tempts us to focus on ourselves rather than entirely on God. As Teresa says in her treatment of the fifth dwelling places, we are to dispose ourselves to be like soft wax for God to impress with any form or shape God so wishes.[12]

I close this chapter with a poem that captures much of the gentle, tender manner of God's ways with us when we find ourselves in the fourth dwelling places, the first stage of this new way of relating, and also in the later ones. His patience, deep respect, even reverence for us, is remarkable and so moving while we learn to trust more and more fully until that day when we know the joy of belonging to him totally.

12. *IC*, V, 2, 13.

COVENANT[13]

> God knocks at my door seeking a home for his Son. Rent is cheap, I say.
>> I don't want to rent. I want to buy, says God.
> I'm not sure I want to sell, but you might come in to look around.
>> I think I will, says God.
> I might let you have a room or two.
>> I like it, says God. I'll take two. You might decide to give me more someday. I can wait, says God.
> I'd like to give you more, but it's a bit difficult. I need some space for me.
>> I know, says God, but I'll wait. I like what I see.
> Hmmm, maybe I can let you have another room. I really don't need it that much.
>> Thanks, says God, I'll take it. I like what I see.
> I'd like to give you the whole house, but I'm not sure.
>> Think on it, says God, I wouldn't put you out. Your house would be mine and my Son would live in it. You'd have more space than you'd ever had before.
> I don't understand at all.
>> I know, says God, but I can't tell you about that. You'll have to discover it for yourself. That can happen only if you let me have the whole house.
> A bit risky, I say.
>> Yes, says God, but try me.
> I'm not sure—I'll let you know.
>> I can wait, says God. I like what I see.

IN CONCLUSION

To be freed and exalted by the Lord, then, we must first be humbled and trust the risen, victorious Christ to help us face with hope and courage whatever is our situation requiring repentance, conversion, and healing. Great love for Jesus, experienced especially during personal prayer, and trust in the guidance he offers in his teachings, will eventually win the day. That day will open us up to new depths, deeper encounters, and moments of union mystical in nature. They hint at a communion with God called, in the classical sense, spiritual marriage. God's Holy Spirit will intensify these sacred moments sometimes. These are what the fifth dwelling places highlight and what we will now explore.

13. Halaska, "Covenant," 357.

QUESTIONS FOR DISCUSSION AND FAITH-SHARING

- What excites you about the ways of praying and new freedoms described in this chapter? What desires do they stir in you?

- Do you have a relationship with anyone with whom you can be silent for long periods of time and simply enjoy being with that person? Do you find God in those moments?

- Have you experienced the kind of prayer described above as praying with the interior senses of your soul? What has that been like for you?

- Do you know someone who has undergone the kind of dramatic conversion like Fr. Newman (described above) was blessed with? What was that like? Where did it happen? During a retreat or when in nature, etc?

9

The Fifth Dwelling Places

THE GOD OF JESUS, the risen One, is a God of amazing surprises. I never tire of reflecting on or talking with others about how true this is. Most of the surprises in prayer characteristic of these fifth dwelling places are subtle. The following example is a dramatic one, letting us see more readily some of the traits of these delicate gifts of God. It manifests faithful, even heroic, love and is lived out in a place of great vulnerability.

AN EXAMPLE

Sister Claudia is a missionary who has served in South Sudan for some years. She lives with the people of that civil-war-torn nation and shares in their fears of being raped, tortured, and killed. She has been shot at a few times and once even dodged a tank shell falling near her, its impact knocking her flat and kicking up gravel that dug into the skin of one of her legs while she was running away with her defenseless people. On that occasion she lived with them in the bush for numerous days, surviving on tree leaves, roots of wild plants, and drinking water from the marshlands that had been filtered through the skirts of the women. Eventually, she and they were rescued by UN peacekeepers. Over many months the villagers had come to observe her closely and eventually adopted her as one of their own. One day a villager asked her why she left her much better, safer way of life to live with them "in our hell." She simply smiled in reply. The villager then declared, "We know that God exists and loves us because you love us." Sister Claudia could never have hoped for a more poignant testimonial. What a blessing and affirmation by God as well!

In her moments of quiet contemplative prayer, Sister Claudia experiences the typical fluctuations of distractions and sometimes periods of being wonderfully centered in God. But lately she has been experiencing a few powerful moments of deep union with God, more powerful than anything she has experienced before. In the midst of the intense heat, the blowing sand, the boredom of the same food all the time—beans, rice, and ugali—and the threat of armed robbers, Sister Claudia becomes completely caught up in God, as if she were seized by him. She is completely abstracted from herself and her surroundings and held in wonder for a minute or two. Even when she returns to an awareness of her body and surroundings, she feels like she is in a cloud, dazed yet deeply comforted and reassured by God, quite taken by such spiritual sweetness.[1] It seems she has sipped of the sweet wine of God!

Over the next few days she wonders whether it is really God she is experiencing or an aberration reflecting the stress of her surroundings. But days later, she feels surprised again during her prayer time, captured by God, completely surrendered to his will. It is impossible now for her to doubt the reality of what is happening. She *knows* it is God who entered the center of her being and let her drink the intoxicating wine of his sweet love. She was in God and God was in her.[2] How exquisite, simply too much for words! She senses like never before how real God is, indescribably tender, good, and beautiful. From her depths she weeps tears of joy and is filled with love, not only for God, but also for these people caught in tribal and political upheaval. Clearly, the people of South Sudan are living the passion of Jesus, nailed to their situation with no means for escaping. She could never abandon them; too much does she love them and Jesus crucified. She is filled with awe at what is being shown her: the broken Heart of God pouring out love in the face of the sufferings of these people.

This is the God who deserves infinite love in return, a truth she appreciates so well now, while at the same time she recognizes how no creature or all of creation by itself could ever give such love. Everything in her longs to find a way to love God to the extent God deserves being loved, that is, infinitely. At

---

1. See *IC*, V, 1, 4–9.
2. See *IC*, V, 1, 9.

the same time, she experiences how miserably inadequate she is, because of her human limits, to be able to realize this longing. At times she catches a hint of Jesus feeling helpless during his last minutes of life, thirsting to love the Father and us with all that he was/is, yet having no sense of this desire being realized! She feels a deep union with him through her suffering and in spirit lays her head on his Heart. She is filled with the desire to someday love God with the infinite love of God, but in the meanwhile do whatever God wants of her for these people, including suffering with and for them.

INCREASED SENSE OF SINFULNESS

At the same time, she feels paradoxically a sharper-than-usual sense of her own failures to love. She is aware of temptations to harbor feelings of anger and thoughts of revenge toward the soldiers who bribe, oppress, and sometimes rape these people of South Sudan. She is disgusted with her own inclinations to violence.

A more mundane example of her failure to love is a petty situation: a tendency to think unkindly about a certain colleague. She is humbled by this awareness, and saddened that she is slighting God, who deserves much better. His love for her makes this weakness, this coldness of heart, more obvious. She so wants to live for God, to do his will, yet this part of her heart still waits for his healing touch. Being prone to old sinful habits and deceits of the evil one, she knows her only way to peace is to depend completely on God's merciful goodness and compassion.

DIVINE RECONSTRUCTION

It is with visitations like these Sr. Claudia experienced that God sometimes blesses those in the fifth dwelling places. Many times his visitations are of lesser intensity but still characterized as surprising moments of union. Whatever the case, God's purpose is to "reconstruct the self into its true divine image . . . [and make us] pay more attention than ever to ourselves, as God, 'like a devouring fire,' lights up hidden corners and exposes within our finitude all that resists 'the calling of the infinite.'"[3] What God provokes, then, is a purification much deeper and more refined. In earlier dwelling places the focus was more on the need for a change in behaviors. Now the

---

3. Seelaus, *Distractions in Prayer*, 57.

focus is on purifying the roots of our behaviors where some un-Christlike attitudes and values still hold sway. We are being given, more than ever, the desire to want what God wants for us.

This reconstruction phase of our journey to God is critical for our transformation in Christ. It was first prepared for in the fourth dwelling places, intensified in the fifth, and will be completed during the very demanding sixth dwelling places through what John of the Cross calls the dark night of the spirit.[4] During the fifth dwelling places, God sensitizes us to anything superficial, to empty distractions, and to idle curiosities of the secular culture. Deeper desires and thirsts awaken in us and serve to narrow and thus deepen the cares of our spirit, opening us to a much more intimate engagement with God, people, and life. Like iron near a strong magnet, we are powerfully drawn to whatever relates to and enriches the precious relationship we have with Abba and Jesus. Like St. Paul, we feel a certain disinterest and perhaps even contempt for what we formerly valued so highly and on which we spent so much time.

God is becoming, more than ever, the one great love and interest of our life. Our new self, as part of a we, is emerging. We are more and more sharing with God one life.

EXPANDED VIEW OF THE TRUE SELF
LIVING WITH CHRIST IN GOD

Diagram 4: Closer View of Our True Self Hidden in Christ

4. See John of the Cross, *Dark Night*, bk. II, chs. 5–10. Hereafter, John of the Cross, *Dark Night*, II, 5–10.

In this deepening union, we see as God sees, feel as God feels, love what God loves, and desire what God desires. We are growing in the habit of thinking and choosing as God would think and choose, yet we are more human and alive, more our true self, than we could have ever asked for or imagined (Gal 2:19b–20; Eph 3:20).

One further aspect of the mystery unfolding here is Divine Love opening us to a new depth of trust and surrender to God, allowing God to lead us to greater humility and self-knowledge. The fire of such love alone frees us to want to know our truth and where we still need the Savior's liberating action to work inside us. We can also better anticipate from a distance the newly transformed self at the center of our castle, where Teresa says Christ the King awaits us. Whether we are blessed with the prayer of union or not, this new sensitivity to who we are in Christ "move[s us] to loving others as God loves them—with God's own love . . . [and allows us to uncover and heal] self-centered concerns that [still] inhibit love and cause disquiet of heart."[5] We are having, increasingly, one will with God.

NOT REWARDS BUT FURTHER HELPS

In the fifth dwelling places, Sister Claudia experiences wonderful gifts thanks to God's visitations. They are given not as rewards for her remarkable service in South Sudan but as helps to overcome failures to love because God loves her so deeply for who she is, his beloved daughter. She is ready now for such blessings and new freedoms. Despite her knowing well her shortcomings, she can live with peace about her unfinished state of soul because of his unconditional love. She walks more surrendered to his mercy and is more patient with his ways regarding her. This gift of understanding God's way of relating helps her toward accepting herself as she is now. She trusts that God sees deeper than these obstacles to the core of who she is.

A NEW WAY TO LOVE SELF

As Sister Claudia continues to face her failures and shortcomings, she is learning to engage in a form of prayer that uses inner dialogue. The method involves an imagined dialogue with any part of herself out of harmony with the deeper desires of her heart. Borrowing from the techniques of Roberto

---

5. Seelaus, *Distractions in Prayer*, 60.

Assagioli's system of *Psychosynthesis*,[6] Sister Claudia focuses intently on an alienating or distracting feeling and lets it express itself. With eyes closed, she converses with this part of herself; first allowing it to speak, to say what is its name (e.g., Karla), and express what it needs (e.g., to be acknowledged, respected, or listened to and eventually welcomed, known, and loved). In other words, she begins not by speaking but by listening and receiving whatever is the truth of any part of herself that has been ignored or denied and needs to be acknowledged and accepted. To do so is to receive and to love herself, in her truth.

She recognizes how it is from this part of herself that she can get defensive, caught in a moment of vanity and competitiveness, or engaged in uncharitable judgments or a gesture of impatience with the tendency to make critical comments about people whose mannerisms irritate her. If she is honest and brave enough to look at these behaviors and attitudes, and more importantly acknowledge them as part of herself, she will then have a sure pathway to Jesus about her need for healing, for his mercy and guidance. Having a total relationship with God requires, as in this example, being transparent with him about our self, and being committed to bringing *everything* to him in prayer. It is the proven way to deeper union with Christ and to experiencing peace and inner harmony with others, God, and our self.

The Carmelite scholar Vilma Seelaus makes a very interesting observation about how God, during our adult years, leads us to a purification of and freeing from our more subtle obstacles.[7] These especially get confronted in the fifth dwelling places, she says. In early adulthood we develop our talents, make choices and commitments, and set personal goals. She cites how we seek independence and self-sufficiency in relation to others who may disapprove. These efforts are normal, healthy, and are important goals in our lives, yet self-possession (autonomy) can, she says, be:

> easily tainted with self-love and self-will . . . It can leave us with a superficial self-understanding based on real or imagined achievements . . . A sense of self, based on our achievements, is often realized at the expense of others. As we climb over our peers up the ladder of success, the temptation to consider ourselves better than others is seldom absent . . . we can stay stuck within the imperatives of success, efficiency, or serving the power interests of

6. See Roberto Assagioli's fundamental works: *Psychosynthesis, The Act of the Will,* and *Transpersonal Development.*

7. See Seelaus, *Distractions in Prayer,* 54.

others . . . our sense of self [can become] increasingly fluid and . . . shift with the expectations of others.[8]

If we are to grow into the later dwelling places, it is critically important that we recognize and work with such inclinations. Not acknowledging these dynamics largely explains why many stagnate in the third dwelling places. Some people can live their entire lives with their career and achievements as the basis of their identity. Like the rich young man, they can live the commandments, yet not grow significantly in the Spirit of Christ.

SURROUNDED BY UNCONDITIONAL DIVINE LOVE

It is worth noting that while the apostles were attracted to Jesus as the new king of Israel, as well as to his anticipated prestige, success, and political power, Jesus still loved them unconditionally. Even when they were spiritually blind and deaf to their attachments, right up to the day they were blessed with freedom from them, he loved them unconditionally. Jesus' loving patience and passion prepared them for their transformation, their Copernican revolution, when the Spirit of Pentecost would come on them. We, too, are invited to desire and trust that this same marvelous transformation awaits us.

Yet, when we find ourselves in these fifth dwelling places, we will be focused not so much on this future hope but more occupied with being lovingly present to God and relating to others as God does. We will be becoming more compassionate, more understanding of our neighbor and of our own self too; we will see hints of the Christ-mystery unfolding in us and feel more secure that, in God's timing, all we hope for will be given.

The exquisite blessings of the prayer of union help us to identify with the words of St. Paul: "I know [the One in] whom I have believed" (2 Tim 1:12). We can find ourselves saying something like: "I *know* him, I have truly met him; he is so very real. I not only have faith in him, but I have *experienced* him, directly and undeniably." These surprises of God in the prayer of union, blessed with a strong sense of certitude that it is God who acted in us, reflect some of what Ignatius of Loyola describes: to "smell and . . . taste the infinite fragrance and sweetness of the Divinity."[9] They help us to identify with and savor more Scriptures like the Song of Songs,

8. Seelaus, *Distractions in Prayer,* 54–55.

9. Fleming, *Draw Me into Your Friendship,* para. 124.

the lyrical passages in Isaiah 40–44, and the poetry of St. John of the Cross. They especially give us a new, stronger sense of wanting to please God in every respect, eager to do his will in every moment.

Teresa emphasizes we can do nothing on our own to make happen this experience of precious union between God and our self. It is God and only God, she says, who can bring this about in us. It is his will to come or not come into the center of our spirit, whenever he desires and as he desires.[10] But she adds that we can dispose ourselves for such a great gift, first by being genuinely resigned to God's will in our life, and secondly by living with a universal love and care for our neighbor.[11]

LIKE A BEAUTIFUL BUTTERFLY

Teresa of Avila is a consummate artist with images. She uses them well to capture the essence of spiritual realities. While the soul likened to a castle is probably her best-known image, her next-best-known image is that of the butterfly, which she uses to represent the state of our soul in these fifth dwelling places. Being likened to the butterfly helps us appreciate how beautiful we have become in this stage of spiritual transformation; yet, at the same time, we are still quite fragile. We are still relative beginners in the spiritual journey and need much more transformation than what has been realized so far.[12]

Our spiritual transformation at this stage is likened by Teresa to the metamorphosis of a silkworm. The silkworm begins its process by feeding on the leaves of a mulberry tree. Once it has had its fill, it spins a cocoon to cover itself. Some weeks later it dies to its old, ugly form and emerges as a beautiful butterfly. Teresa likens the cocoon to Christ who, by giving himself to us in the prayer of union, becomes a protective house where all that is un-Christlike in us can die: self-love, self-will, and other attachments. This miracle of transformation happens thanks to God attracting us to himself, first in the fourth dwelling places through the prayer of active recollection and later the prayer of quiet, but finally and especially in the fifth dwelling places, through the prayer of union. We are given with this exquisite kind of prayer, Teresa says, an increased desire to love Christ and to show this love in prayer and virtuous deeds.

10. See *IC*, V, 1, 12.

11. See *IC*, V, 1, 9 & 2, 1.

12. See *IC*, V, 2, 1–8.

FRUIT OF THIS TRANSFORMATION

> From the fifth [dwelling places] emerge simple counsels chiseled on the heart like 'Thy will be done.' [Or 'My food is to do the will of him who sent me' . . . or, . . . 'not my will but yours be done.'] Many virtues come to fruition, especially humility or walking in [the] truth of who we are. Another is detachment from anything or anyone that overly preoccupies us so that we can become like clear panes of glass through which rays of divine light shine. Mutual love can also be exercised in many ways, ranging from almsgiving to . . . words of encouragement when someone feels low.[13]

Acts of generosity coming from a gifted heart, like boldness in leaving safety and security behind to give ourselves in love, or being transparent without concern for loss of esteem, testify to our loving God very deeply. Teresa stresses the importance of these acts of ordinary charity. She says they are spiritually more significant to our growth in Christ than the extraordinary experiences of union in these fifth dwelling places.

Teresa says the special intimacy with Christ given in the prayer of union leaves us with a deeply joyous feeling that we belong to Christ. We become, she says, like softened wax totally available to him to be shaped however he wills; he has put his seal upon us.[14] Yet, this intimacy exposes us to some struggles and pains (e.g., feeling more estranged than ever from earthly things; wanting to enter heaven but having to stay in this life; sensing we are still not totally given to God and in danger of losing this gift by misplaced affections; and lastly, grieving over many who seem in great danger of being eternally lost). We have "to persevere in relinquishment and the inmost yielding of [our] will to him . . . *to hold on to nothing but God and to everything in God.*"[15] We are involved in a courtship that will lead hopefully to a betrothal, which is described in the sixth dwelling places. Teresa firmly counsels that this stage of growth demands of us fidelity and vigilance about such delicate gifts given so far. Discernment especially is necessary for avoiding deception and staying close to Christ. She also emphasizes continuous growth in the virtues, doing our ordinary obligations with increasing love, and being more ready to be taken as least among others.

13. Muto, *Where Lovers Meet*, 70.

14. See *IC*, V, 12.

15. Muto, *Where Lovers Meet*, 64 (emphasis original).

The butterfly image represents, then, new, more loving behaviors rooted in attitudes and values in harmony with the Heart of Christ. Its delicate nature, however, suggests that some concerns for our self still affect us. Overall, it represents what is called:

> a beginning of perfection, [not perfection itself] . . . A long, long journey lies ahead involving great struggles. There will be falls, there will be some blindness for the soul . . . [During our time in the fifth dwelling places our soul] is . . . tested and prepared for the Bridegroom's personal visit. [We get the sense] not only of who he is but of what it is going to mean to have him as spouse.[16]

BECOMING AS GOD

According to Henri Nouwen in his *The Return of the Prodigal Son*, we all have alive in us the wandering, sensual prodigal son, as well as the envious, judgmental, and self-righteous older brother. Hence the need for the last two dwelling places and their unique gifts. Till we acknowledge and have mercy on both brothers in us, we cannot live the spirituality of the father. As Nouwen so movingly explains, becoming like the father implies we would "allow the sins of the world to pierce our heart and make us shed many, many tears for them"[17]; we would be constantly forgiving and giving ourselves away without reserve. This would be to live out of a "sacred emptiness of non-demanding love."[18]

Does not this description of the Father describe God so well? How awesome that God is giving us himself, his Heart, his all in this way, especially in the later dwelling places. Our hope is to grow into the qualities of heart and spirit described of the Father and eventually be divinized, transformed and empowered to live and love as God does, while being utterly humble, full of joy, and pouring ourselves out to him and all creation without any fears or limitations.

---

16. Burrows, *Fire upon the Earth*, 84–85.

17. Nouwen, *Return of the Prodigal Son*, 128–33.

18. Nouwen, *Return of the Prodigal Son*, 133.

THE GREAT IMPORTANCE OF LOVING OUR NEIGHBOR

There is need to stress, though it was briefly stated above, that Teresa says that deeds of love, of care and sacrifice for our neighbor, are more important and determinative of our spiritual growth than any experiences of the prayer of union. She likens our failures to love our neighbor to the silkworm not dying in the cocoon, not becoming a butterfly, but instead, chewing away at our virtues and minimizing any progress.[19] Self-esteem, not wanting to lose any of our rights, and being judgmental toward others, even in minor ways, she says, especially undermine progress. Loving our neighbor will express what is of the essence of these fifth dwelling places: a "union with Jesus in his death,"[20] exercised in self-abnegation, especially in faith, patience, trust, forgiveness, letting go of control, and in the turning of our will again and again to God. Our will is being transformed to desire Christ with our whole being, "the one thing necessary" (Luke 10:42), to give the underground River of Divine Life total freedom in our self. The blessings of these dwelling places constitute, then, "a dynamic moment of decision, an invitation offered and accepted, understanding that this acceptance is beyond our power and is a direct effect of God's contact."[21] God, then, has brought about this new freedom by evoking the desire to want only God and the longing to give everything to him. This gift given becomes a certain foolishness of love, as St. Paul would call it (1 Cor 4:9–13), the will to lose our self in the Beloved. Yet, paradoxically, it leads to finding our real self, our deepest truth and beauty.

IN CONCLUSION

It is quite humbling to learn that those who live in these fifth dwelling places are still relative beginners in the spiritual journey. This truth is largely because the so-called lower operations of the soul (i.e., the senses and imagination, the intellect and memory) are not yet coordinated or in harmony with the will.

19. See *IC*, V, 3, 6.
20. Burrows, *Fire upon the Earth*, 88.
21. Burrows, *Fire upon the Earth*, 83.

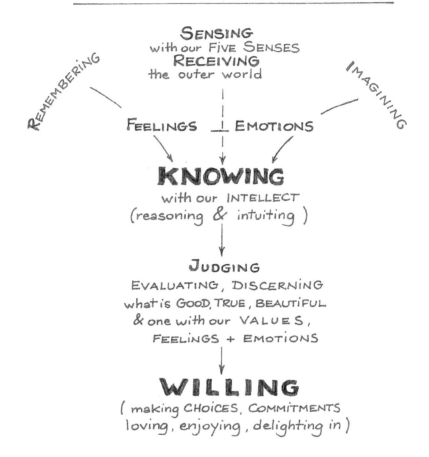

Diagram 5: "Operations of Our Soul"

The will in these fifth dwelling places has been strongly attracted by God to God and powerfully moved, much more than before, to want to love God with all that one is.

> [But] the will is not made to work alone. To have its full power and accomplish a lasting work, it and the lower [operations of the soul] must work together as a team. Unfortunately, these [operations] not only scarcely sustain it, but even pull it in the opposite

110

direction. They are [at times] . . . selfish and rebellious. What can the pilot of a ship do if his crew is not trained, or refuses to work?[22]

Much work is left, then, on God's part, in cooperation with us, before we are fully integrated and our entire psyche is brought to unity and peace. This is specifically the focus and work of God in the sixth dwelling places.

Amazingly, Teresa spends more time in *The Interior Castle* on these sixth dwelling places, with their eleven chapters, than on any others. Clearly, she is keenly interested in this stage of God's deep, radical work of bringing our entire person into an abiding union with him. In them, she says, God will betroth us, preparing us for the day when he will marry us (Isa 62:5). Such preparations will involve significant trials and sufferings, not unlike what Jesus anticipated at the Last Supper. Identifying with him in Luke 22:15, we will find ourselves desiring to progressively increasing degrees, a new depth of communion with God and neighbor. It is the fire of the Holy Spirit or underground River of Divine Life that will carry us through this most challenging of all the dwelling places.

QUESTIONS FOR DISCUSSION AND FAITH-SHARING

- What for you was the most beautiful part of what Sr. Claudia was given directly by God, and then by God through the people she was serving?

- How would you explain to others the metaphor of the butterfly? What is the significance of its delicacy, its fragility?

- Share in a group the results of each member using the exercise called "disidentification" presented in Assagioli's *Psychosynthesis*. Use it as a way of identifying those parts of yourself needing healing and reconciliation with your core self.

- Can you relate to the language of friendship, betrothal, and marriage with God when recognizing the deeper desires of your own soul? If not, how would you speak about these stages of intimacy between you and Abba (Amma)/Christ Jesus?

- Are you struck by or attracted to Henri Nouwen's description of God in his relating to his two sons: one the prodigal, the other the judgmental and resentful son? What specifically do you admire/love in God the Father as described by Nouwen?

22. Madeleine of St. Joseph, *Within the Castle*, 113.

10

The Sixth Dwelling Places

IN THE SIXTH DWELLING places Teresa gives a detailed account of the climax of a conversion process that has been going on since the beginnings of what was described in chapter 5 as a spiritual Copernican revolution. Here, Teresa describes God's purifying actions as more intense and demanding than in any of the previous dwelling places. In the third and fourth dwelling places, we began to appreciate how remarkably self-focused we were. There we were awakened to, perhaps shocked by, how the seven capital sins, with our ego and self-centered inclinations, were still quite alive in us. Divine Love enlightened us with self-knowledge, gave us courage to acknowledge and face this part of ourselves, and blessed us with significant detachments and new freedoms. As St. John of the Cross says in his *Ascent of Mount Carmel*, book I, chapter fourteen, we were "fired by love's urgent longings"[1] to experience a love for God stronger than the loves we had for our false gods.

Teresa demonstrates this transformation by showing how God draws us beyond the limits of self into what she calls divine espousals, to increasingly profound, intimate experiences of him so that we can be much more centered in him. We are won over from attachments like "the myth of self-fulfillment . . . taints of ego-inflation and self-centeredness . . . subtle forms of 'vanity,' as well as 'arrogance' and ineptitude: . . . residual pride lingering

---

1. See John of the Cross, *Ascent of Mount Carmel*, Book I, ch. 14.

deep in the spirit . . . [and covering over] our innate insecurity [in the face of this awareness] with a veneer of superiority, or spiritual excellence."[2]

THE SPECIFICS OF GOD'S TRANSFORMING WORK

In the fifth dwelling places we were freed to truly want whatever God wants. But deeper interior work needs to be done in these sixth dwelling places: namely, a radical reordering of the functions of our soul so that not only will our will work steadily in union with God but so, too, all the other functions named in Diagram 5. God brings our senses, emotions, or affections, memory, imagination, intellect or understanding, and intuition into harmony with him and with our will. We are freed from opposing impulses, biological and psychological included. This healing and interior integration is an extraordinary gift! God does this by:

> mobiliz[ing] the intellect and the subconscious itself . . . by a direct action that will be both illuminating and effective. We are moved with delight and great affection and illuminated about spiritual mysteries. Our feelings are re-aligned "to feel with Christ, like Christ . . . [and to be] entirely devoted to the Father . . . capable of going to the Father as he did—spontaneously, with [our] whole being. It means receiving this movement of Christ present in the deepest part of [our] heart [as our own].[3]

Besides the realignment and harmonization of the operations of our soul, there will be some additional, extraordinary gifts fit for the betrothed of Christ: especially a great expansion of our soul's powers to be poured out like Jesus and the Three Divine Persons. We will be loving with divine *agape* as our own, made capable of loving with a depth greater than ever before. This will ready us for the life of abiding union with Christ, a state of soul Teresa calls the seventh and last set of dwelling places. But first, a more extensive treatment of God's deep work in the sixth dwelling places.

MYSTICAL FAVORS

Teresa spends eleven chapters explaining the drama of the sixth set of dwelling places. Seven of these chapters are devoted to explaining the

2. Seelaus, *Distractions in Prayer,* 92.
3. Madeleine of St. Joseph, *Within the Castle,* 144–45.

extraordinary mystical blessings she received in this stage, and two chapters detail the effects of such experiences. She mentions locutions, raptures (also called ecstasies or transports/flights of one's spirit), visions, and blows or piercings like an arrow to the soul. Indeed, these are very rare blessings, and many who come to this stage of spiritual development do not experience them. They are well worth our consideration, however, because knowing about them deepens our awe for God's power working in our depths, and our respect for the variety of ways God can transform us in Christ. It also helps us to appreciate God as *the* consummate artist when glimpsing something of our being recreated in Christ.

Locutions are words heard within our spirit. They give insight and direction. One of the more famous instances of this is the experience of Francis of Assisi (d. 1226) at the extensively damaged church of San Damiano near Assisi when he heard Jesus speaking to him through the cross: "Francis, go and repair my house [church] which, as you see, is falling completely into ruin."[4] This event proved to be a conversion moment for Francis and his becoming one of the greatest figures of church reform.

Locutions can also be erroneously imagined to be spoken by God, or they can be spoken by a spirit masking as God. Teresa says locutions from God bear good fruit; like peace, certitude, and inner delight. They effect what they say (e.g, the locution "trust me" can be immensely strengthening when one is subjected to great trials of darkness and doubt). The Evil One can feign certitude but not give deep peace or light.[5] Discernment, therefore, is very important.

With *raptures* God suddenly seizes us, lifts us out of our senses, and places us very close to him. Our will is absorbed and our intellect suspended; we are completely focused on the Beloved and given great enlightenment by a direct, sudden communication.[6]

Teresa describes a special kind of rapture, seemingly like what St. Paul experienced when he was lifted up into the third level of heaven (2 Cor 12). This she calls a "flight of one's spirit," being carried off suddenly, very quickly by God. She likens it to being in a little boat while riding a huge wave that took her where it willed.[7] All she could do, she says, is surrender to God's power and will, to let the wave carry her. She further describes

4. Bonaventure, *Bonaventure*, 191.

5. See *IC*, VI, 3, 5–17.

6. See *IC*, VI, 11, 4.

7. See *IC*, VI, 5, 3.

how her soul in this experience was being inundated with "the waters of God," flooded with God's blessings while at the same time being made quite aware of her weaknesses, faults, and failings. She emphasizes it takes great courage to endure these experiences because of the suffering that goes with being much more sensitive to how imperfect you still are when compared to God's holiness and love. The grandeur of God overwhelms us with how powerful God is, leaving us with much less esteem for earthly things. How like the experience of St. Paul in Philippians 3:7–8, who reevaluated everything as "a loss" once he had experienced Jesus so profoundly on the road to Damascus! These last three blessings (knowledge of the grandeur of God, self-knowledge and humility, and little esteem for earthly things) are what Teresa calls the jewels Christ as Spouse begins to give to the betrothed.[8] This impact of God sometimes makes one want to die and go to God.[9] Our only desire is to be with God and gaze with love on him in pure contemplation and serve him out of immense gratitude, wanting even to suffer for him.[10]

Visions can be intellectual, imaginative, or sensory in nature. The first kind is much more trustworthy as coming from God, less liable to deception.[11] Teresa gives an example from her own prayer, saying she strongly sensed Christ at her side, yet saw nothing. She says this experience gave her deep peace, an abiding desire to please God, and a complete lack of interest in anything that would not bring her to him. These blessings assured her these visions were from God.

Another example of this kind of a vision is what happened to St. Ignatius of Loyola (d. 1556). While living as an ascetic at Manresa, Spain, many years before he founded the Jesuits, Ignatius was sitting one day near the River Cardoner, and suddenly "the eyes of his understanding began to be opened; though he did not see an [imaginative] vision he understood and knew many things and matters of faith and of learning, and this was so great an enlightenment that everything seemed new to him."[12] He later said in this moment he saw or found God in all things and all things in God, learning more about God than he did in his seven years of theology studies at the University of Paris. This vision would profoundly shape the way he would relate to God and the spirituality he would offer the church and world.

---

8. See *IC*, VI, 5, 10–11.

9. See *IC*, VI, 6, 1.

10. See *IC*, VI, 11, 7.

11. See *IC*, VI, 8, 2–3.

12. Ignatius of Loyola, *Autobiography of St. Ignatius Loyola*, 39.

Imaginative visions, on the other hand, can more readily be the product of our own imagination manipulated into a sensory-based experience. In both kinds of visions Teresa strongly counsels discussing these experiences with a competent spiritual guide. Unless there is a basic humility on our part and wanting only what God wants, any claims of visions are suspect. Teresa says it is far safer for spiritual growth not to receive or seek visions but to grow more by receiving the delights (*gustos*) given by God in contemplation.[13]

Another mystical favor Teresa mentions is *a blow or piercing of the soul*, as with an arrow. She says this happened to her when feeling intensely the desire to be fully and finally united with God, yet having to wait for this union. This longing and ache consumed her entirely. Much of her yearning was in feeling caught between earthly things necessary for living this life, while seeing the One she so loved at such a distance. She was unable to climb to God, nor get to the "waters of God."[14] She says only a further vision or rapture given by God can relieve this torturous dilemma. Its intensity is dangerous to the body, even life-threatening, unless it is relieved after a few hours.

One other kind of experience, dangerous to the person's life, can be *a joy or delight so vehement* that it makes the soul swoon and tend to leave their body. This can put the person in danger of death, so heavy is the impact of God.[15] The Bernini sculpture of Teresa of Avila in ecstasy, pierced with an arrow, suggests something like this.

WHAT IS ESSENTIAL?

Many who are led by God into these sixth dwelling places do not experience the extraordinary mystical gifts that Teresa of Avila did. This fact tells us that spectacular gifts like those described above are not essential to the deep work God is doing in these advanced souls. We must ask then: What is essential to realizing the blessings of transformation distinctive of the sixth dwelling places? Teresa tells us God wants anyone in these dwelling places to desire more intensely than ever before entering total, complete union with Christ: to want to be alone with and live in complete conformity to him as one's All. We must want to be rid of anything that might block this betrothal but, above all, to entrust one's entire self to God's initiatives.[16]

13. See *IC*, VI, 11, 9.

14. See *IC*, VI, 11, 5.

15. See *IC*, VI, 11, 11.

16. See Muto, *Where Lovers Meet*, 76–77.

God's method, then, is basically the same as it has been in all these dwelling places: to arouse desires for him while allowing us to undergo experiences that serve to purify our motivation, values, and attitudes. In other words, "God [makes] room for God by [wooing us with what Ignatius of Loyola calls spiritual consolations and] by illuminating the clutter of things we still cling to . . . enticing us to deeper humility and freedom of spirit through painful experiences of [our] imperfections and sinful tendencies."[17] These are what St. Ignatius calls desolations. By way of a back-and-forth of favors and trials, then, God purifies and deepens us.

Teresa describes her most intense experiences as "blessed madness,"[18] when God ravished her with both the sweet and the painful. True to the pattern in earlier dwelling places, these exalted blessings come with a very high cost while readying us for the seventh and final set of dwelling places. It is only fitting that such a treasure would cost everything in the drama of Christ and us coming to know and love each other with all we have and are! Such a union is beyond anything we could anticipate. St. Paul says as much in one of his letters: "What no eye has seen, nor ear heard, nor has [our] heart conceived, what God has prepared for those who love him" (1 Cor 2:9).

Teresa's way to such intimacy was prepared for through terrible sufferings, especially through people in her Carmelite order and priests and bishops giving her much grief. She was the object of gossip and rumors, some quite critical, with some alleging she was trying to make herself out to be a saint and judging that she was extreme and dangerous to the spiritual welfare of others. These detractors would tell priest confessors, "Everything [about her prayer] is . . . from the devil or melancholy."[19] Because of this she feared these priests would be unwilling to hear her confessions. With some others, she was the object of great praise, which embarrassed her enormously since she knew anything good in her was from the indescribable kindness and generosity of God. Eventually, she felt a freedom to disregard these comments, whether spoken with contempt or exaggerated praise. She could see the providential hand of God allowing such persecutions to purify her soul and make her find her peace and joy only in God.[20]

Teresa suffered also for more than forty years from poor health. Sometimes her physical illnesses were quite serious, contributing to mental,

---

17. Seelaus, *Distractions in Prayer*, 84.

18. See *IC*, VI, 6, 10.

19. See *IC*, VI, 1, 8.

20. See *IC*, VI, 1, 3–13.

psychological, and spiritual sufferings. At times she says she would have chosen martyrdom over these pains. They greatly exercised her patience.[21]

Worse than the physical sufferings was the guidance she was given by an inexperienced priest, who she says was much too careful and unable to trust anything but the predictable. It truly hurt her to be judged negatively and suspect when sharing some of her extraordinary experiences. He thought that since she was less perfect than an angel, it was unlikely she could receive such extraordinary blessings from God.[22]

In addition to this suffering was her anxiety over possibly misleading her confessor, thanks to what she said was an inability to explain well her unusual experiences. She struggled to discern the truth of God in it all, imagined spiritual disaster for herself thanks to deceits of the Evil One, and feared that God was abandoning her. Efforts by other confessors to help her made her state of soul only worse, leaving her feeling terribly alone. She could not pray and was subject to excruciating temptations that she had no love for God nor ever had any; that all her previous favors had been conjured up and that God had turned his back on her.[23]

COMPLETE SURRENDER

The most important gift God led her to through such sufferings, and to anyone else in these sixth dwelling places, was complete surrender and trust in his initiatives. She was learning how powerless she was to realize anything good, and how important was this humbling knowledge about herself for what was ahead of her. The only response that made any sense to her was "to engage in external works of charity and to hope in the mercy of God . . ."[24]

These extreme sufferings were terribly trying when at the same time she felt, deeper than all this pain, an overwhelming attraction to Christ and desire for total union with him. Sometimes she felt like she was being torn apart, like Jesus in the garden of Gethsemane. She felt abandoned and lost, yet God was also wounding her again and again with his incomparable love. Divine Love counseled her to accept it all, these sufferings and sweet divine visitations, and go on with her day. She learned to resist any inclination to

21. See *IC*, VI, 1, 7.
22. See *IC*, VI, 1, 8.
23. See *IC*, VI, 1, 9–11, and 13.
24. *IC*, VI, 1, 13.

justify herself, whether in the face of condemnation or high praise, and instead only to forgive and love.[25] She had no ability to understand what was happening to her or what was being given to her. It was beyond anything she could have imagined or invented. It was all God's doing!

Earlier I said the mystical favors given to Teresa are not essential to God's transformative work in the sixth dwelling places. I offer three brief profiles of individuals who did not experience the mystical gifts Teresa of Avila did but who experienced an intimacy and depth of relationship with God characteristic of those in these sixth dwelling places.

THREE EXAMPLES

Perhaps the best-known example is that of the popular Carmelite saint, Thérèse of Lisieux (d. 1897). During her twenty-four years of life, she did not enjoy any of the mystical favors Teresa of Avila did. God led her differently to awesome wisdom through the Scriptures, contemplative prayer, and the great sufferings that Thérèse offered especially for those who had lost their faith. God's forming her intensified and climaxed in the last six months of her life when Thérèse was dying of tuberculosis. Through it she suffered what many consider a classic case of the dark night of the spirit, feeling utterly abandoned by God, similar to some of Teresa of Avila's experiences. Specific to this taste of hell on earth was her temptation to fear that there is nothing at all after death.[26] Yet, the practical, down-to-earth wisdom in the writings of this young woman, some of it dictated during her last months, and the great fruit realized in the lives of countless others, witness strongly to the power of God thanks to her radical trust in him. Many people turn to her in prayer for God's help and guidance.

Another example is found in the Old Testament prophet Jeremiah, whose vocation and relationship with God was, from the beginning, a struggle filled with conflict. Jeremiah was often outspoken with God, complaining and demanding from God what he needed for fulfilling his mission. He tells how the Word of God burned within his depths (Jer 20:9), that he found these touches of God sweet to his spirit, so much so that he says he "devoured" God's Word (15:16). At other times he blames God for deceiving or seducing him (20:7) into a very trying mission, that God's captivating love left him no escape. Threats of death, feelings of failure in the

---

25. See Muto, *Where Lovers Meet*, 77.

26. See Miller, *Trial of Faith*.

face of Israel's disappointing response to God, and temptations to despair (Lam 3:1–20), while at the same time being so in love with God and his fellow Israelites, reveal a man so authentic, holy, and purified of any will of his own. He is an excellent image of God passionate for relationship with us and willing to suffer for it.

One of my favorite examples of someone encountering both the blessings and trials distinctive of the sixth dwelling places is the largely unknown Italian, Anna Maria Redi (d. 1770).[27] She joined the Carmelites in Florence, Italy once she turned eighteen, leaving her family of eleven. Her father underwent a kind of Gethsemane experience when his favorite child and closest soul-friend chose the cloister. From the time Anna Maria was three years old she would frequently ask adults, "Who is God?" It was obvious that very early on God had destined her for something truly special.

Taking the religious name of Teresa Margaret of the Sacred Heart of Jesus, Anna Maria served as the monastery's infirmarian for her fellow sisters. In the fewer than five years she lived as a Carmelite, she experienced a great intensification of her search for God. She suffered significantly as God moved deeply in her, making her sensitive like few others to the delicacy and demands of his love so pure, so worthy of total response, and then infinitely more. Teresa Margaret felt these very strong divine initiatives pressing on her, moving in her, opening her through frequent spiritual direction and the Sacrament of Reconciliation to vehement longings to give herself to God totally and completely. On Trinity Sunday, 1767, two years before she died, Teresa Margaret encountered God in a way and with a depth she never had before. She was stunned and mesmerized by a divine touch so powerful that it left her for many days in a trance. Her fellow sisters could tell from her demeanor that something soul-shaking had happened. Teresa Margaret had experienced the answer to her lifelong question: now she knew *throughout her entire being* that God is Love. Reflecting the beauty of her religious name, Teresa Margaret of the Sacred Heart of Jesus, she desired with everything in her to live hidden in the Heart of Jesus, alone with him, she said, "as in a desert." From that sacred space she would be led into the depths and joys of the Triune God, but only after an intense and extended dark night.

Even though she died suddenly of a bowel obstruction, her spiritual guide said that in all truth her death "was caused more by the secret violence of love than by her short illness, or perhaps, the illness was caused by the

27. See Rowe, *God Is Love*, 217.

force of her love."[28] The weight of Divinity over against the woeful limits of human flesh was too much for her to bear any longer, and so it was time for her finally to come home to the One she had been searching to know and love since she was three years old. Miraculously, her body did not decompose after death and can be viewed today, as I have been blessed to see, at the Monastery of St. Teresa of Jesus on the Via dei Bruni in Florence, Italy.

OTHER BRIEF EXAMPLES

Three religious Carmelite women and a biblical prophet may seem to be esoteric examples of those who pass through the sixth dwelling places. John of the Cross is of the opinion that God takes very few people through this stage while on earth. Who knows whether he is right or not? The sufferings of the twentieth and twenty-first centuries and the thousands of victims and martyrs of war and religious persecution, most of them unknown but to a very few, leave me wondering whether this miracle of transformation and surrender to God characteristic of those in this advanced stage is more common than we would expect.

It seems St. Mother Teresa of Calcutta is one example: living for fifty years with a deep darkness and severe dryness in her prayer yet finding God readily in her ministry to the dying wretches of the streets of Kolkata, India. Toward the end of her life, she came to appreciate how God, in allowing her to feel so abandoned and empty in her prayer, was revealing to her something of what those dying in the streets of Kolkata experience,[29] as well as what Jesus experienced when hanging on the cross (Ps 22).

St. Oscar Romero, martyred in El Salvador in 1980, is another example. After being a quiet seminary professor for many years, he was elected archbishop for the church in his nation and was immediately thrown into the chaos of a civil war. He soon gained a strong sense of the cry of many of his people: farmers too poor to own their own houses and land, and too poor to send their children to school. On weekly Sunday radio he would plead with the well-to-do families for fairness, compassion, and justice toward those working on their plantations. This enraged most of these families and those holding political power. The final weeks of his life were something like the final days of Jesus' own. He experienced intense fears

---

28. Gabriel of St. Mary Magdelene, *From the Sacred Heart to the Trinity,* 89.

29. See Mother Teresa, *Mother Teresa.*

and nightmares while waiting for the inevitable, his death by assassination. Romero was silenced with a bullet through his heart while praying Mass.[30]

Walter Ciszek (d. 1984), an American Jesuit priest, is another example of the depths of God's transforming work in the sixth dwelling places. In 1939, Ciszek went to Russia with high hopes of bringing spiritual strength to this nation subjected to the cruel, atheistic ideology of the communists. Instead, he was arrested under suspicion of being a Vatican spy. For nearly three years, during the worst of World War II, he was interrogated every day by the secret police or KGB, pressured to confess that he was a spy for the Vatican. Having come to Russia to give his all to God, Ciszek, in a moment of profound mental exhaustion, signed the confession the Soviets wanted. Within a few minutes, he collapsed psychologically, shouting out bitter statements of self-hatred and furious anger toward God. Providentially, that moment in his purgatorial ordeal became the turning point of his life.[31] He came to understand that God above all wanted him to hand himself, mind and will, over to him. God was setting him free from his plans for serving God the way he thought God wanted and, in their place, Ciszek was to trust God in each *present* moment to reveal whatever would be the next step in it. He finally understood that God wanted him to love the Russian people as they were: suffering greatly under police-state circumstances that sought to crush all religious expression. Above all, God wanted him, *in each present moment*, to be entirely abandoned or surrendered to him, receptive to whatever God wanted. Over the next twenty-one years, Ciszek would live with this new remarkable freedom of spirit before returning to the USA in 1963. He could say then, more than ever, "I live, no longer I, but Christ lives in me" (Gal 2:20).

Prayer for a person in the sixth dwelling places originates far more from the initiatives of God than anything coming from his or her thoughts, desires, or memories. The only contribution of the person is his or her consent to whatever God gives and wants, even though the person often does not understand its meaning nor see the blessings that will be forthcoming. This state of soul is what St. John of the Cross calls the dark night of the spirit (i.e., God bringing to light, more clearly than ever, the inclinations to evil still alive inside a person, while at the same time giving them an unprecedented sense of his infinite holiness). The contrast between God and themselves, John says, can weigh so heavily on them that they can be

---

30. See Brockman, *Romero*.
31. See Ciszek and Flaherty, *He Leadeth Me*.

tempted to despair, hardly able to pray vocally, and prompted to put their face to the ground in great humility and wait for God to lift them up.[32]

PERHAPS MANY OTHER EXAMPLES

I strongly suspect there are among us numerous people of remarkable spiritual growth and transformation as described in these sixth dwelling places. How typical of God to work such miracles of grace in hidden ways, leading generous souls of his choosing to heights of great Christlike holiness. I like to think we will discover among them some who lived the vocation of marriage and family with great, even singular, sacrifice; some who underwent terrible suffering thanks to being orphaned or widowed early in their lives; or suffered the humiliation of a divorce or were chronically weak thanks to a longterm illness; some who find themselves to be of homosexual or lesbian orientation and encounter verbal and psychological abuse as well as exclusion because of it; those who are falsely accused and have lost their reputation, their financial reserve, and their health because of the stress of being socially ostracized.

I am sure that when Christ brings us home to be part of his new creation, to join his family, we will be filled with boundless amazement at how the providential, transformative power of God was realized in our own lives and in those of many others. We will be full of praise when recognizing how God is *the* divine Michelangelo, as shown in the beauty of our new self and in the beauty of our recreated neighbor. We will hear each other's stories of how God accomplished this in us, of how the victory of divine merciful love has become the last chapter of each of our stories. We will be filled with joy and wonder at his wisdom, creativity, and enduring love. We are becoming far more than we could have ever asked for or imagined (Eph 3:20).

Now it is time to look at the seventh and last of Teresa's stages of spiritual growth, the moment when, alleluia, the spiritual marriage begins.

QUESTIONS FOR DISCUSSION AND FAITH-SHARING

- From the many examples/profiles in this chapter, which examples strike/touch you the most? Why those?

32. See John of the Cross, *Dark Night*, II, 5–8.

- Do you know the story of anyone who has recently lived, or is now living, through a lot of suffering and has come closer to God in the midst of it? Do they show any of the extraordinary qualities of soul that St. Teresa or others profiled in this chapter showed? Which qualities?

- Might you consider it an opportunity for a great spiritual deepening in yourself by living out your last days in a nursing home while more and more surrendering everything to God? What might that be like for you or anyone who is close to Christ Jesus?

11

The Seventh Dwelling Places

WHEN WE PONDER THE extraordinary favors and very heavy trials experienced during the sixth dwelling places, it seems at first glance that the blessings and manner of life for those in the seventh dwelling places are rather
ordinary. This seems to be the case because they lack the drama and great
swings of joys and sufferings of the previous set. One commentator com-
pares the experiences in the sixth and seventh dwelling places to wind and
storm over against "gentle rain, silent and penetrating."[1] Yet on further
analysis of these seventh dwelling places we are amazed at the quality and
depth, the uniqueness even, of the gifts distinctive of the glorious climax
to our journey home to God and to the center of our soul. They are more
developed and more mature than those of the sixth dwelling places.

THE BEST OF GIFTS

The gift of all the gifts in this final stage is the *abiding* presence of the love
of Teresa's life, the risen Jesus who has been waiting for her at the center of
her soul. "The heart of Christ is now her abiding place of rest,"[2] with its
fullness and quality of presence unlike any other she was previously capable

---

1. Madeleine of St. Joseph, *Within the Castle*, 193.
2. Seelaus, *Distractions in Prayer*, 131.

of receiving. Here all is marked by simplicity, her total ease with Christ, and Christ with her.

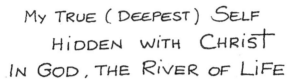

Diagram 6: Our True Self in the Heart of Christ

She tastes and savors what she calls the vintage wine of God reserved for those welcomed by Christ to the secret and deepest cellar of the interior castle.[3] Teresa describes Jesus at her center, or wine cellar, as "the King" reigning in his palace.[4] The two of them, she says, rejoice together in deepest silence, while now she feels free from her former fears, especially those experienced in the sixth dwelling places. With his presence comes a peace and joy much deeper than what she experienced in any of the previous dwelling places. She struggles to express how much richer and fulfilling is this gift.

3. See *IC*, VII, 4, 11.
4. See *IC*, VII, 2, 11.

We get some clarity when she describes how, with a deep intuitive vision, she sees the God of Three Persons making his home permanently in her soul. While she undoubtedly sees and has some understanding, thanks to this direct gift from God, the faculties of her soul, blinded and deafened by this divine intervention, are stunned, amazed at what God is doing, and do not understand anything of this divine intervention.[5] She describes how her life, with its great joy, likened in the fifth dwelling places to a fragile but gorgeous butterfly, has grown so far beyond that auspicious beginning and now is Christ.[6] She so appreciates this awesome mystery at her deepest center because now she experiences very often certain powerful aspirations that move in her and prompt her frequently to respond with immense love. She says they are like a "full-flowing river," the underground River of Life referred to early in this book, giving off "spurts of water" that feed and sustain her mind and will, etc.[7] She adds, "there is Someone in the interior depths who shoots these arrows and gives life to this life, and there is a Sun in the interior of the soul from which a brilliant light proceeds and is sent to the faculties."[8]

These divine initiatives are truly unprecedented. Teresa is saying she is experiencing more than ever who she is, her true self, her uniqueness found in her relationship with the risen Christ. To live in and for him, whether it is in this life or the next, is all she wants. All that matters is that they are together now and forever. Whether explicitly conscious of him or not during her day, still, deeply united with his will, she can go about loving others, doing good works, as he modeled and commanded (John 15:12).

UNIMAGINABLE INTIMACY WITH GOD

The greatest effect of this transformation in Christ is her being led into the joy and freedom that God enjoys within the life of the Trinity. The Three Persons enable her to live the life of God as her own life. She is left breathless at the beauty and spiritual sweetness of this eternal, without a beginning, total self-giving of the Divine Persons. Never had she seen or tasted in her depths anything as beautiful as this. As each of the Divine Persons is completely surrendered in the outpouring of his being and love

5. See *IC*, VII, 1, 5 & 3, 11.
6. See *IC*, VII, 2, 5.
7. See *IC*, VII, 2, 6.
8. *IC*, VII, 2, 6.

for the other two, so the human person in the seventh dwelling places is blessed in two special ways: letting go of everything about herself or himself and, second, entrusting everything to the Divine Bridegroom in this new and joyous spiritual marriage. We are so taken by the divine Other that we are no longer aware of our self, taken beyond all self-consciousness, and lost in the beauty, goodness, and truth of him, the precious Beloved. We have come to the fullness of what we are destined for in Christ: living and moving in the unending joy of God, being treated as an equal in this glorious communion with the Triune God. All this because of Jesus. He is the door to this fullness, "the Master of all of [our] affection,"[9] the only way into such a communion with God. We are completely inner-directed and harmonized with God's promptings, seeing and experiencing from these center rooms what God sees and experiences. "An inner light indicates the direction that will keep [us] on the path of total self-gift."[10]

CHRIST IS HER ALL; SHE HIS ALL

Christ has said to Teresa, "All that I have now belongs to you, and I will take care of whatever is yours."[11] As the perfect bride, she surrenders all into the embrace of Christ, the perfect bridegroom. There is no other attachment to anything anymore, except to Christ. Her one and only interest becomes loving and serving him, even in the smallest of things. If there is any fear on her part, it is about the possibility of failing him, a fear of the slightest discourtesy. She even wishes to suffer for him, if possible, but is detached about that possibility.[12] With this desire is an unmistakable joy when she is persecuted because in such an experience she knows a profound union with him who suffered for her, while also feeling compassion for those who persecute her.

She now knows the joy of giving everything, of pouring out her entire person to the only One who can receive all her heart and soul; just as Jesus knew it in giving himself entirely in the Eucharist and on Calvary—to us and for us, yes, but supremely so to Abba Father. Each of them, Teresa and the risen Christ, gives his or her total attention to the other as well as to the cares and concerns of the other. In a sense Teresa becomes Jesus and

9. Madeleine of St. Joseph, *Within the Castle*, 183.

10. Seelaus, *Distractions in Prayer*, 120.

11. *IC*, VII, 2, 1.

12. See *IC*, VII, 3, 4.

he becomes her, the her now transformed in him. She enjoys the privileges of the Divine Person who is Christ, "totally inclined toward the Father."[13] She is empowered to do what God does best: namely, love with the mercy, depth, and purity of God's love shown especially in the crucified Jesus who poured himself out in selfless giving, even for those who executed him.

In one of her analogies used to express the depth of this gift of transformation, Teresa says the union of this marriage with the risen Jesus is "like what happens when rain falls . . . into a river . . . all is water . . . the rain . . . cannot be divided or separated from the water of the river . . . or like when a little stream enters the sea, there is no means of separating the two."[14] How this awareness must be mixed with copious tears of joy!

"It is only when God has been able to love us in fullness that we are wholly *there*. Only that in us which is divine is real. Only when we are God-filled are we truly human."[15] God has brought Teresa, finally, into this indescribably beautiful, ecstatic, joyous state of being, "when nothing of the self remains in possession."[16] She can say with St. Paul, "It is no longer I who live, but Christ lives in me; and the life I now live in the flesh I live by faith in the Son of God, who loved me and gave himself for me" (Gal 2:20). Paradoxically, she is now more than ever the beautiful person she was created to be! The old self *as a self* has died; a new reality has emerged, one of being fully human and fully alive. "The experiential structures of selfhood, on which, in experience, we center ourselves, [fall away . . . and we are recentered by Divine Love] on a ground that is beyond any possibility of experience."[17]

MYSTICAL MARRIAGE, MORE THAN AN IDEALIZED SELF

What is described above, then, tells us of some of the mystical, spiritual marriage Teresa has been talking about. Spiritual marriage implies that we have become more than a fully developed, mature personality or realized some state idealized by various respected psychologies. To be sure, it includes a truly remarkable reordering of the operations of our soul, named in Diagram 5 and explained in the previous chapter. But more to the point,

13. Madeleine of St. Joseph, *Within the Castle*, 184.

14. *IC*, VII, 2, 4.

15. Burrows, *Fire upon the Earth*, 112.

16. Burrows, *Fire upon the Earth*, 112.

17. Denys Turner, quoted in Seelaus, *Distractions in Prayer*, 133.

this new state is about being totally given to the Divine Other, poured out just as Jesus was/is entirely poured out to the Father. "[It] is [for] those who are totally hidden and lost in God, living only with the life of Christ . . . [and being] Fire on earth."[18] It is a blessed state inaccessible except to those who are drunk on the wine of Christ. One's state of life does not matter: religious, cleric, or lay. What does matter is our being totally given to Jesus and to the Father, while allowing the risen Jesus Christ to live more and more in us. More specifically, Christ's risen life in us is marked by his loving the Father with boundless depths, while receiving the Father who loves the Christ emerging more and more in us.

"What constitutes us as persons and . . . gives us identity is not the body/psyche existence that is uniquely ours but our relationship with God."[19] We move toward becoming our true self when, in imitation of our Creator, we give ourselves away to God and neighbor in selfless love. We find our true self, then, only when we are fully part of a "we" constituted by God and our self.

NOT YET HEAVEN

It must be emphasized that this state of profound union of God and Teresa was not free from troubles in Teresa's work world, in her carrying out responsibilities, or in dealing with difficult people. It is in the person's faculties (i.e., their mind and memory, their imagination and will, with its role in making decisions, also in their senses and passions) where the person in the seventh dwelling places gets challenged and burdened.[20] This fact heightens our awareness of the soul's center as distinct from any of its operations. It is in this core of the person, what Teresa calls the "essential part of her soul,"[21] where the extraordinarily graced person of the seventh dwelling places is unshakably established in Christ and his peace. This amazing effect makes it abundantly clear that it is God who has brought about this rocklike stability in the person, something the Evil One could never feign.

Our focus, then, even if challenged in the soul's operations, will be on loving Christ and doing good works, on bringing great love for him to whatever we do, rather than focusing on our discomforts, concerns, or

18. Burrows, *Fire upon the Earth*, 118.

19. Seelaus, *Distractions in Prayer*, 131.

20. See *IC*, VII, 2, 10.

21. *IC*, VII, 1, 10.

desire for greater psychological wholeness. All hell may swirl around us, and yet at the same time this fact reminds us of how fragile and vulnerable humanity is until the end of our earthly journey. Till the moment we pass into eternity, no matter how far God has taken us into the ways of holiness, there can stir in us at times echoes of our own concupiscence. In this life we are never above or beyond the human condition. What is so reassuring, however, is the divine power that can save us, without any loss of peace, in all situations tempting us to sin: this is what Teresa experienced in the "essential part" of her soul.

This fact of sin-prone humanity prompts Teresa many times in *The Interior Castle*, especially in her treatment of the sixth dwelling places, to urge us strongly that in this life we need to stay focused on the humanity of Christ, no matter how mystical or advanced our prayer and spiritual growth become. Jesus, the Christ, grounds us in the reality of our humanity and dependence on Abba Father and the Holy Spirit. That is the way it is in this earthly life and will be in the next. In this life, except for visions one might or might not be given as in the sixth dwelling places, we will be given what is entirely an intuitive, loving awareness of Christ in the Triune God. In our prayer we will more likely not be aware that it is Christ with whom we share intimate communion. But afterwards, upon reflection, we will most probably have a sense that it is he who was/is present to us. This great gift orients us during our day to see life and all of reality through his Heart and eyes. "His is the face . . . present in our consciousness as his life is secretly, escaping our consciousness, substituting itself for ours. We are becoming Jesus . . . [with] his own wisdom infused into depths we cannot see."[22]

THE ESSENCE IS SURRENDERING TO LOVE

From the fourth dwelling places to the seventh we learn, especially during prayer, to practice surrendering to God, letting God be God, trusting God more and more radically. This is what is called the prayer of *being* distinct from the prayer of *doing*. We let God be God and vigilantly wait, trusting and loving him. This characterizes the way Jesus related to his Abba. Surrendering to and trusting in God is, above all, who Jesus is. It makes so much sense for our eventually experiencing a profound harmony between our spirit and Jesus' Spirit that our focus be given exclusively to him, the

---

22. Burrows, *Fire upon the Earth*, 108.

God-Man. We enter through his Heart into the infinite, bottomless depths of Divinity. Over time:

> Jesus is effecting his own surrender in us, drawing us away from all self-interest, beyond any effort to become the ideal person, and wooing us to make his love ours. It is a profound sharing in his death, but a death that is only the reverse of life . . . [often we struggle] to accept and be happy and content in this "poor" existence. We can't see that this, embraced with love, *is* union with God. It is to be in [him who is] the Way [and] is always *there* in the heart of God.[23]

Toward the close of Teresa's masterpiece, she counsels her sisters (and us) to "Fix your eyes on the Crucified [one] and everything will become small for you [and us]."[24] This saying underscores how the human Jesus/ risen Christ is indispensable in finding our way into the heart and depths of God. She insists this is the only way for a Christian to experience healing and lasting freedom from our fears and empowerment in the midst of our limitations and powerlessness. We are urged to gaze at length on him, the great I AM, in whose name is salvation for *everyone* who believes (John 6:40). In John 4:47–53, there is a touching example of this possibility, when, like what Teresa counsels, we "look on him and believe." In this story a Roman official, a Gentile, begs healing from Jesus for his dying son and is given what he requests but then much more: his whole household is blessed with the gift of faith in this compassionate, very human Jesus as divine.[25]

CONCLUSION

With Teresa of Avila's *The Interior Castle* as a guide, I have offered a contemporary exposition of seven stages of spiritual growth in the life of the human person, illustrated from my own pastoral and personal experiences. We followed Teresa's vivid, sometimes very detailed, description of the unfolding of the human soul. We saw how noteworthy God's method is

---

23. Burrows, *Fire upon the Earth*, 108–9 (emphasis original).

24. *IC*, VII, 4, 8.

25. This is what Jesus counsels in this sequence of texts from St. John's Gospel: 3:14, 8:28, 12:32; 19:37; and 20:28. They all testify to Jesus being lifted up on the cross or being pierced by the soldier's lance. We are to look intently at him there and accept the invitation to place our hand in his open side, and on the wounds to his hands and feet, and come to belief in him as the great "I AM."

for effecting this unfolding: the steady and increasingly strong attractions to God, through Jesus, while we journey from surface, sometimes sinful, levels of living to deeper and more authentic levels of our self. We experience through this exodus the emergence of our deepest and most authentic desires. Eventually our soul is opened to want only one thing as our deepest desire: Christ Jesus, the risen Lord, "the one thing necessary" (Luke 10:38–42). Through him, God harmonizes the human soul with all that is good, true, and beautiful in creation but above all with himself, the Father, Son, and Holy Spirit.

The apostles Peter, James, and John, when with Jesus on Mount Tabor, were graced to witness in Jesus' transfiguration a manifestation of his divine depths. His divinity radiated with intense refulgence, overwhelming them for a while. What also left them speechless was their being blessed to see how everyone who puts faith in Christ will someday in God's future, like Jesus, be transfigured in Christ and manifest these same divine depths.[26] Our destiny as children of God, and the longings of all creation for this freedom and glory, will have been fulfilled (Rom 8:21–23). Praised be Jesus Christ! Praised be the most holy and glorious Trinity, now and forever. Amen!!

QUESTIONS FOR DISCUSSION AND FAITH-SHARING

- How might you explain or image the "essential part of our soul" and represent in connection with it the other operations of our soul? (See Diagram 5 in the conclusion of chapter 9.) What function of the soul expresses the "essential part of our soul?"

- What does the "wine of Christ/God" suggest to you about the way we are destined to be with and relate to God? And being "fire on Earth": what does this suggest to you? Does it remind you of anyone?

---

26. Downey, *Altogether Gift*, 98–102.

SECTION IV

Highlighting Implications

12

Foundational Issues in Spiritual Growth

IN THE FINAL THREE chapters, I will explore further the overall theme of this book: the journey toward realizing our deepest desires. These core desires are implied in Teresa of Avila's *The Interior Castle*. When providing spiritual guidance, I have noticed that certain core desires in the spiritual journey keep surfacing, explicitly or implicitly. Regardless of age, gender, or racial or ethnic background, I hear the same basic needs and desires being expressed in:

- the need to be accepted and loved by others
- the need to accept myself as I am, as someone good and lovable
- the need to live my life as worthwhile, as it is, and with hope that it can become more
- the longing to give of myself and make a difference in the lives of others
- the desire for meaning and happiness in my life as well as in my work
- the desire to understand what God is doing in my life and for what purpose
- the desire to learn how to pray and grow into a great love for God
- the need to find meaning in suffering that leads to growth, peace, and compassion
- the need to forgive, heal, and reconcile.

Many people seek me out for spiritual guidance because I point them to something different from, but which often complements, what a counselor or psychologist offers: namely, the way of Christ and how they can cooperate with his Holy Spirit in realizing one or more of the core needs and desires cited above. At the same time, I am sometimes helped in my own journey by their stories. In them God gives me certain pearls of wisdom that I can share with others as well.

THE SEARCH FOR LOVE AND MEANING

What impresses me most in these stories is the universality of this human search for love and meaning, to be wanted and cared about. Nothing means anything to us if there is not some genuine human love in our life. Otherwise, we feel less than human and disconnected from life. I have learned that our deepest need is to be accepted and respected for who we are, regardless of how incomplete, inadequate, or flawed we may be. Our worst suffering is to be abandoned, dismissed, shamed, disowned, cut off, and told to go away. It can be a living hell to suffer such rejection.

Likewise, it is not possible to enjoy trusting relationships unless we are loved for who we are and can relate in love to others. Being valued as a person worth being loved is, from my experience, the cornerstone of a healthy spiritual and emotional life. Otherwise, we look for love in various wrong places (e.g., in possessions, in what we do, in the favorable opinions of others, and in manipulating those whom we want rewards from). To become the person we have been created to be we must experience love from God and caring human beings. We are especially blessed if we can recognize and own, like Jesus did at his baptism, God affirming us as his beloved on whom his favor rests (Matt 3:17).

THE CHALLENGE TO SELF-ACCEPTANCE

What emerges in these stories as the greatest struggle, more than the need to be accepted by others, is the need to accept our own self *as we are*. For many this blessing can require significant struggle. Complementing our being able to accept and love ourselves *as we are* is the longing to give of ourselves and make a notable difference in the lives of others. Our peace, happiness, and fulfillment in our search for meaning, depend greatly on realizing these foundational needs/desires. This developmental issue plays itself out well, usually in those who have a loving parent, loyal friend, or teacher praising and encouraging them, especially during their formative years. I am convinced that all healing depends on our having a positive attitude toward our self. If we are not accepting of ourselves, if we are wishing we were someone more successful and praised, then this lack of basic self-love gets projected on others and makes us more likely to wound rather than love. Good counseling and good psychology can go a long way toward fostering healthy self-acceptance. Their contributions are greatly deepened when we encounter the crucified, risen Christ, unconditionally loving us for who we are, and calling us to be part of his mission. Being loved and accepted by Christ, then, and experiencing ourselves making a difference when giving ourselves to others in love, saves us from death and opens us to eternal life.

A STORY OF RECONCILIATION

I remember, as an example of the power of such love, the story of an African woman retreatant I guided. I will call her Sr. Marcia. She spoke about the tender love she experienced as a small child from her dearly loved father when he would often give her hugs and, while she was seated on his lap, let her eat from his plate during meal times. During her teens, however, she was devastated when he brought home a second wife while still married to her mother. Sr. Marcia, by now in her late forties, confessed she could not be consoled until years later when, on his deathbed, her father apologized and was reconciled to her, to her mother, and to Christ. His polygamous choice could not erase from Sr. Marcia's heart the lifegiving sweetness of his love for her as his little girl. The love they had for each other served as the locus of Christ's love calling him home, like the prodigal son, to his truth as a Christian. It was a call to reclaim his identity as a husband married in Christ to one woman, and as a father to this faithfully loving daughter. Like the father of the prodigal son, his daughter could not forget the joy she knew with him from their earliest days. Love given became love given back and mutually life-giving. In the end, their truth, shared in Christ, won the day.

I recognized in this woman's account the mystery of Christ's resurrection happening not only in her father but in her as well. It was preceded by her participation, sometimes rather intense and for more than thirty years, in the sufferings of Jesus during his passion. The meaning she found, thanks to forgiving her father and healing with him, deeply changed the way she could now be with herself and the people of her life. It was an instance of the resurrection mystery happening right before my eyes. I was so blessed to see in her face and hear in her voice God's tender, merciful care shining through, as well as her unforgettable joy in this long-awaited victory of suffering love. God's Holy Spirit had given her who was now conformed to Christ crucified the strength to persevere all those years. Her love bore a similarity to Christ's own distinctive love: faithful to the love that had united them years ago and ready to give everything for the other.

Yes, divine love is this powerful. It is the most powerful energy in all existence. It is the only power greater than death and our only hope for helping us, like Lazarus, to remove the wrappings holding us in our tombs. If only we could let God work this power in our lives! It would surely move us from whatever dwelling places we may be in to the next set, especially from the third to the fourth, with its pivotal Copernican spiritual revolution as explained in chapter 5.

GROWTH THROUGH LIABILITIES

In the stories I have been blessed to hear I often witness instances of what I briefly alluded to above: the universal struggle to accept our own human reality; of being limited, of coming from this family and not another, of being "only me" and not someone else more successful, more attractive physically or personality-wise, more talented and less dependent. What we consider to be a liability can be experienced as such when, for example, we are growing old and are not able to do what we used to do; or we pray for years for a certain favor or healing and do not perceive any answer; or we try to overcome some nagging, embarrassing fault, but sense no change or resolution. Our becoming spiritually mature, more like Christ, depends very much on what our attitude is toward these so-called liabilities: whether we embrace them with trust in Jesus risen as *the* way for coming closer to God; or, sadly, we try to avoid them as much as possible. Jesus' way for living with our humanity, with its limitations and vulnerability, is highlighted in his eight Beatitudes. They are wisdom statements, often experienced as counter-cultural, and show us the way to our being transformed in him, to realizing our deepest desires.

BECOMING POOR IN SPIRIT

The first of the Beatitudes encapsules the other seven. It says: *blessed are the poor in spirit; theirs is the kingdom of heaven.* In it Jesus encourages a humble acceptance of ourselves as we are, as loved sinners, and trust radically in God's promise to be our strength and salvation in each present moment. It gives depth and perseverance to our faith, hope, and love, the three foundational virtues of Christian life, especially during our more formidable spiritual struggles. For St. Teresa of Avila, it describes humility and declares its fruit, i.e., God's welcome into his peace and joy, not just in the future but also in the present moment.

The wisdom and challenge of living this first beatitude have come home rather strongly to me in recent years when feeling my body aging, yet at the same time feeling quite alive spiritually and psychologically. I am touched with increasing wonder and gratitude for my life, but also find myself inspired to entrust everything to him, especially intimations of my mortality and having to let go of what I was formerly able to do. I am well aware that these are invitations to accept who I am in that moment. I simply have to say "yes" to it all and trust. This is what being "poor in spirit" or "empty" before him looks like, while letting him make whatever he wishes out of it.

A SECOND STORY: FINDING STRENGTH IN WEAKNESS

I vividly recall a man named Andrew telling me how often he has to surrender to God the reality of his family of origin. Frequently he gets tempted to much worry and loss of hope about his chronically angry, alcoholic mother and alcoholic, often unemployed brothers who have fathered children by various women and have on-again, off-again relationships with them. His bigger spiritual challenge is to accept himself coming from this family with extensive dysfunction and self-hate among its members. When he hears about other families whose members have college degrees and jobs and everyone seemingly enjoying life, he feels like a failure, ashamed of his family and tempted to be envious of what the "successful" ones have. He feels sometimes a certain aloneness, but especially the temptation to blame God for the whole situation and not believe in himself and God's love for him and his family. As St. Teresa would counsel, Andrew needs to pray from this place of turmoil and feeling abandoned and bring to God his sufferings or spiritual poverty, particularly his anger toward God, and beg for greater faith and trust in the risen Christ's merciful promise of salvation. The resurrection hardly feels real to him. He identifies more with the pain of Good Friday.

EXPRESSIONS OF THIS HUMAN POVERTY

Some of the more common expressions of this state of our poverty, of being just me and not someone more acceptable, are the following:[1]

- being perceived as rather ordinary, therefore unnoticed, not appreciated;
- being exceptional, standing out among many, and perceived as a threat to others; I hide my gifts and try to be seen as like everyone else;
- being in need, physically or psychologically, therefore unable to provide for myself; having to beg; feeling incomplete or inexperienced;
- being a stranger in a foreign culture, not able to speak very well the local language;
- feeling impatient about my life and its future, risking failure or criticism;
- experiencing the loss of other possibilities once I choose one possibility (e.g., being married to *this* person, being given *these* children; or being a member of a religious congregation and having to live with some disagreeable members);
- having a kind of work that is boring but must be tolerated because I am the sole provider;
- being in a church community led by a pastor who micro-manages and leaves little room for the creativity, generosity, and call to ministry of its members.

These experiences suggest and prepare us for our death, the ultimate expression of our human poverty. Our mortality prepares us to accept ourself as completely dependent on God, while believing that we are destined by this most loving, divine parent for something awesomely wonderful.

More immediate than our mortality in reminding us of our humble state is how poor we often are in our efforts to accept our powerlessness and

---

1. I am indebted to Johannes Metz's *Poverty of Spirit* for a number of these insights into spiritual poverty.

dependence.[2] Until we die concupiscence, or the tendency to any of the seven capital sins, will prompt our most acute temptation: to flee these experiences of our human vulnerability and powerlessness, to deny even having them, or fill them up with some distraction, an idol of material wealth, or a self-centered pleasure. We must allow ourselves to be freed from our need to control our life. Usually it is a loss, failure, humiliation, or a time of foolishness that shakes us free from chasing these empty possibilities and helps us meet the real God: on the cross where we see God experiencing in Jesus what we undergo. There, as in a mirror, we see ourselves. There with his love and compassion he waits to embrace us in our poverty. He knows that our human vulnerability oftentimes frightens us and so often he says to us gently but firmly, "It is I whom you are experiencing in your vulnerability. Courage! Do not be afraid!"

Our strength, then, is the strength of God revealed in weakness. "There is something about God that is better expressed in weakness than in strength, in foolishness than in wisdom, in poverty than in riches."[3] I have frequently witnessed this power, the victory of the risen Christ, manifest in the joy, laughter, and great sense of companionship among people exiting an Alcoholics Anonymous meeting. They had shared with each other their weaknesses, their shame and guilt, and need for a Higher Power. They felt great freedom as a consequence. Even though they might avoid using explicitly religious language, they find Christ and hope among each other. Whether they say they believe in him or not, the resurrected Christ is in their midst, helping them grow toward accepting themselves as loved and welcomed as they are. This process of shared weakness and self-humbling brings many alcoholics out of their tombs. Often it frees them to believe in God's personal love and acceptance of them, veiled and mediated by a community struggling with the same cross.

GOD'S WAY OF SAVING US

"The story of the earthly Jesus Christ is a story of human failure, of human poverty, of human foolishness"[4] but breakthrough to victory. God comes to us, not in spite of these experiences but precisely in and through them.

2. I am also indebted for the following insights on spiritual poverty and the first beatitude to Simon Tugwell's *The Beatitudes*.

3. Tugwell, *Beatitudes*, 2.

4. Tugwell, *Beatitudes*, 2.

They constitute God's way of saving the world, a method that is often judged as insane by those ready to advise God on a common-sense approach for saving humanity. Calvary is where God's wisdom is so powerfully manifest in the face of a world, and too often a church, that wants to say a loud no to it all. Too often we want the glory of the Easter event while bypassing everything involved with Good Friday. It is only when dealing with the limiting, humbling realities of our body, psyche, and spirit, of our marriages, families, and religious communities, that we begin to see the wisdom of God's ways and experience the amazing power that is given to us from the pierced Heart of Christ.

Our journey to God requires our learning to live with our weaknesses and nonachievements, and being willing to learn from any knowledge gained from our poverty and human imperfections. Cooperating with God in his freeing us requires resisting the temptation of trying to escape from these weaknesses and replace them with something we can accept more readily. Such substitutes are often our trying to accomplish one more success.[5] It is my sense that all sin proceeds ultimately from an unwillingness or inability to believe that we are loved by God right here, right now, *as we are*. Therefore, we do not accept nor are we at peace with ourselves (Rom 14:23). We get willful and are driven to *make* ourselves perfect and lovable. When we try to make it happen, the results become *our* righteousness, *our* achievement, *our* self-made holiness. We become pleased with ourselves rather than being transformed in Christ into something much better, full of God's goodness, and deeply happy.

Sr. Marcia learned much from her powerlessness so she could let go and let God while she waited with heroic hope for her father's reconciliation. So, too, Andrew's struggle with self-acceptance within his family of origin is God's breakthrough into his life, sustaining him with faith and hope.

THE LURE OF SIN

When we choose to follow our own way and wisdom, seeking strength and wholeness according to our common-sense approach, we are much more subject to the promises of the gospel of an unbelieving world. This gospel, with its undue hope in psychologies of human self-improvement and a life seeking wealth and comfort, or with its blind faith in certain social movements, political reforms, and economic causes, can never lead to life.

5. Tugwell, *Beatitudes*, 15.

The former way leads in the direction of a first-world, narcissistic, afflu-ent lifestyle. The latter is often marked with attitudes of anger, resentment, envy, infighting, or even the will to violence. Both ways offer salvation and ultimate meaning, but neither can deliver on its promises. Both set us up for perceiving ourselves as enlightened persons who are superior to others, more conscious and accomplished than the rest.

St. Ignatius of Loyola (d. 1556), founder of the Jesuits, was convinced that the root of all sin is ingratitude, the forgetting of the blessings of God in our life and being blind to how everything is a gift from God. This attitude is often accompanied by the attitudes of entitlement and living as though we are god. Adopting these attitudes for ourself leaves us poorly prepared for coping with spiritual desolation and temptations to many kinds of sins.

The spirit of ingratitude and attitude of entitlement originate from our thinking we are not good enough, from not accepting ourself *as we are*, and envying others; perceiving them to have what will make us more lovable, successful, and esteemed. The book of Wisdom (2:24) explains the origin of sin and fall of the rebellious angels coming from their envying God, of not accepting themselves as they were. Genesis explains the origin of human sin in terms of Adam and Eve envying God, wanting to be equal to God by knowing both good and evil. The murder of Abel by his brother Cain pro-ceeded from envy. So too the building of the Tower of Babel (Gen 11:1–9). Manifest in each of these failures are ingratitude and a refusal to accept our self *as we are*, abundantly blessed by God while still dependent on God.

THE NEED FOR FORGIVENESS AND HEALING

In many stories I have listened to, anger seems to be the dominant emotion that arises when people are trying to heal from past hurts. Sometimes anger reflects impatience or our protesting an injustice. More often it is a symp-tom of being hurt or frustrated or trying to avoid future hurts. As a spiritual guide and retreat director, I often need to give the person permission to express their feelings and help them name and describe the hurt underlying their anger. Next, I explain what they must do, especially through prayer, in order to forgive. I stress that forgiveness and healing is a process, that there are specific steps to it, and it often takes time, sometimes a lot of it. It is humbling and demands self-acceptance; it is being poor in spirit.

THE HUNDREDTH SHEEP COMES HOME

I finish this chapter with a remarkable story of someone who experienced healing from much shame and self-hate, of being forgiven and healed, after living a life of resentment, anger, and cruelty. It is, I believe, a parable of the redemption of us all.

Peter van der Broek, a white South Afrikaner, was the second son of a father who was severe in his standards for recognizing the efforts of others, quick to reprimand, and too much of a perfectionist to praise his children. He never smiled. His mother was quiet by nature, a good woman but too reticent to protect her children against the verbal abuse of their father. Peter, for different reasons, would at times be filled with rage at both parents but much more toward his father, who often left him feeling like a failure, guilty, and lonely. His rage set the tone in his way of being a police officer during the years of the infamous apartheid government of South Africa.

In the face of rebellion and the demonstrations of the racially separated nonwhites, van der Broek and other officers would at times beat, torture, and kill some of them. One evening he and three other officers, while quite drunk, shot and killed at point-blank range the only child, an eighteen-year-old son, of a simple couple, a man and woman much loved and admired by the other villagers. The officers partied while burning his body, turning it over and over till it was reduced to ashes. Five years later, van der Broek, with other officers, came back through the same village, got into an arhument with the father about whether the son deserved to be shot, grabbed and dragged him into a nearby field, built a wood pile and tied him to a stake there, then doused it with gasoline and lit it. Van der Broek and the others, laughed and yelped, slapping their thighs in celebration while the wife heard her husband say, "Dear God, forgive them!"

In 1994, there came tumultuous political change in South Africa. Nelson Mandela, a black citizen who had spent twenty-eight years in prison, became the nation's president. Instead of launching an avenging, anti-white movement, he set up what was called The Truth and Reconciliation Commission. It reviewed cases of injustice and facilitated healing among those victimized by the decades-long racist apartheid regime. Officer van der Broek had his turn to stand before this commission and admit to his crimes. The judges asked the widow who had lost her son and husband at the hand of van der Broek what she wanted from him.

I want three things," she said calmly. "I want Mr. van der Broek to take me to the place where they burned my husband's body. I would like to gather his ashes and give him a decent burial.

Second, Mr. van der Broek took all my family away from me, and I still have a lot of love to give. So twice a month I would like him to come to the ghetto and spend a day with me there so I can be a mother to him.

Third, I would like Mr. van der Broek to know he is forgiven by God and that I forgive him too. I would like to embrace him so he can know my forgiveness is real.

As the elderly woman was led across the courtroom, van der Broek fainted, overwhelmed. Someone began singing, "Amazing Grace." Gradually everyone joined in.[6]

The profound love of this woman, imitating Jesus, who forgave even his murderers, pierced Peter's heart. Her compassion deeply touched the wound that had festered in him since childhood and which had prompted his cruel behavior. For days, while in his prison cell, he wept copiously, and he did the same when out on his biweekly day-leave with the widow in the ghetto. He hardly knew what to say or do when she would hug him. He was like Saul, later St. Paul, changed by a powerful encounter with the risen Christ.

More than a year passed, marked by his twice-a-month visits to the ghetto. One day, Peter, with the little money he was permitted, bought a bouquet of flowers for the elderly widow and two cupcakes with candles to celebrate his birthday. She had nurtured in him self-respect and an acceptance of himself as loved, forgiven, and understood for all that he had been through. He so wanted to tell her of his love and endless gratitude, and profound regret. It was in her that he met Jesus for the first time. Their celebration was truly an *agape* moment for them both and a hint of that first Eucharist when Jesus gave his entire self to his fragile disciples. It was a celebration of van der Broek's birthday but more so of his birth into Christ's life.

Van der Broek had more years to finish his prison term but was now ready to live the new life he had been given through this widow. She was an astounding Christ-figure, with her wounds gloriously shining with divine light in the same way the risen Jesus had shown himself with his wounds to his disciples. Love as mercy and awesome compassion had healed van der Broek's father/mother wound. He was able to forgive his parents from the heart, commend them to God's care, and even forgive himself. He spent

6. Green, "When We Are Reconciled," 11.

the rest of his life, some of it in prison and some outside, telling his story to many of how he had been raised from the dead and, like the first disciples, had seen the risen Lord.

In the next chapter I will present some of the beautiful things God does in and for us when we, like Peter van der Broek, respond with humility and gratitude to such awesome, unmerited love coming from the depths of God, manifest in the pierced and open Heart of the Savior.

QUESTIONS FOR DISCUSSION AND FAITH-SHARING

- What details of the story of Peter van der Broek serve well to make this story a parable of the redemption of us all, a coming home of the one-hundredth sheep?

- Can you relate to any of the issues cited early in this chapter as important points that come up in spiritual direction/individually guided retreats? Also, to one or more of the expressions of our poverty as human beings cited later?

- Can you relate to the struggle with family issues like those presented in the cases of Sr. Marcia or Andrew, or know people who can relate?

13

Becoming a Beloved Disciple

STORIES LIKE THOSE IN the previous chapter can elicit the desire for healing and being loved, totally and unconditionally. They can also inspire
powerful desires to pour out our whole being. Sooner or later in the spiritual journey, with its joys and pains, these core desires for total giving and
total receiving will emerge and open us up to the Infinite. We have been
made ultimately for the Infinite. Our soul will resonate fully only with
this One, like a fingerprint matching a specific finger of a person and no
one else. This chapter reflects on how we can realize this deepest desire
and soul-need of total giving and total receiving with the One who is
Gracious Mystery.

MEETING THE BELOVED DISCIPLE

The history of Christianity testifies to the imitation of the Beloved Disciple
in St. John's Gospel as one of the most fruitful ways for realizing our deepest
desires. One of the favorite images of this disciple pictures him reclining on
the chest of Jesus during the Last Supper (John 13:23). It is there, upon the
Heart of the Savior, we are invited to receive the most extraordinary of gifts
reserved for the closest of Jesus' followers. As we identify with the Beloved
Disciple, we come to know Jesus intimately and to love him profoundly. He

reveals to us the precious secrets and treasures of his Heart, leading to our becoming another Beloved Disciple.

With these special blessings Jesus reveals what Catherine of Siena (d. 1380) says are the secrets of his Heart reserved *just for us*.[1] When we know deeply that we are special to him and known personally, we become more finely tuned to and in harmony with Jesus and his desires. It is here that we fully own the story of his death and resurrection interpreting the meaning of our own life story. In these moments of union, Jesus reveals to us our deeper self, as well as God as our tender, merciful, and ever-welcoming Abba Father.

Many come to such graces by giving special attention to the Gospel accounts of Jesus' passion, death, and resurrection, especially to the pierced side of Jesus. There they enter his Heart to unburden themselves, resting there for long periods of time. Many others come to such blessings by praying with *The Spiritual Exercises of St. Ignatius of Loyola* and focusing particularly on the passion, "labor[ing] with Jesus through all his pain, his struggle, his [physical] suffering . . . [so too] the loneliness, the interior pain of rejection, [being betrayed, denied,] and feeling hated."[2] They taste and see Jesus' personal love for them, "that he willingly suffers everything [because of their] rejections and . . . sins."[3] Some are given even a deep sense of Abba Father's sufferings during the Good Friday event, grieving and weeping with him, compassionating him over the rejection of his most precious Son.

Others dare to enter the Heart of Jesus when he is at prayer and are given an unforgettable sense of the joy, beauty, and overflowing goodness in the total love exchange between him and Abba Father. The Easter stories, Pentecost, and the life of the new church celebrating and proclaiming the risen Christ, especially the manifestations of the Holy Spirit, can open us up to this intimate, loving knowledge.

Powerful encounters of love shown in Jesus' sufferings and joyous resurrection can constitute a fresh discovery of Gracious Mystery, and deepen in us intimations of the immensity and abundance of God's saving love (Eph 3:14–21). They are opportunities for knowing unparalleled love and

1. Catherine of Siena is quoted to have heard God say in her prayer, "I have allowed his (Jesus') side to be pierced in order to reveal the secrets of his Heart, which I have made a hidden refuge where you are permitted to see and taste the ineffable love I have for you" (Glotin, *Sign of Salvation*, 22).

2. Fleming, *Draw Me into Your Friendship*, paras. 149, 151.

3. Fleming, *Draw Me into Your Friendship*, para. 151.

can attract us, with increasing power, into the depths of Jesus' Heart, filling us with an all-consuming fire of love. We are transformed through blessings like these until we live totally, as our own, God's Trinitarian life, in which we give all we have and are to God and in service of our neighbor.

THE JOURNEY OF THE BELOVED DISCIPLE[4]

From the beginning of Jesus' ministry we notice the Beloved Disciple's attraction to and interest in Jesus, how with his brother Andrew he converses with Jesus at length on the first day they meet him (1:35). We do not see him again until the foot-washing scene during the Last Supper (John 13) one to three years later, after being discipled and described as "the one Jesus loved" (13:23). How profound and singularly beautiful must have been their intimate conversations, with Master and disciple touching the depths of God. He, the disciple, encounters Jesus like no other disciple and is blessed with a singular knowledge and profound love. In his Gospel, composing it decades later, he names Jesus as: God's Word or perfect expression (John 1); the new Wine of God's abundance (Chapter 2); the Bread of Life (John 6); the Light of the world (John 8, 9); the Good Shepherd (John 10); the Savior of the world (John 4); and the Resurrection and the Life (John 11), among other titles.

During this most solemn evening, then, he has his feet washed by Jesus as a profound gesture of the Master's humble love for him and as an example of how he and the other apostles were to serve and care for each other. He is the one who leans back on the Heart of Jesus to ask the chilling question about who is Jesus' betrayer (13:23). Like one wanting never to leave the side of his Master/teacher, the Beloved Disciple, once Jesus is arrested, follows Jesus into the courtyard of the high priest (18:15–16) to be with him or as close as possible during his interrogation and incarceration that fateful night. The next morning, we find the Beloved Disciple standing next to Jesus, who is lifted up, nailed to a cross. With Jesus' mother and a few others, he, the only male and the only apostle, stands by Jesus till the very end. In Jesus' last moments this Beloved Disciple is given Mary, Jesus' mother, to be his own mother and to care for her (19:27). He is the Gospel's eyewitness to the piercing of Jesus, calling our attention so movingly to the

---

4. I am indebted to Shea, "Beloved Disciple and the *Spiritual Exercises*," 5–24, for the points he makes about the specific scenes in St. John's Gospel regarding the Beloved Disciple's actions vis-à-vis Jesus.

blood and water flowing from the Heart of the Savior (19:34–35). From the time of Jesus' arrest until the death of Jesus, the Beloved Disciple models so eminently the hoped-for response to Jesus' frequent counsel: "remain with me, dwell in me" (15:4–7, 9).

It is this Beloved Disciple who is the first to have some understanding of the resurrection of Jesus. Early Easter morning, he receives from Mary Magdalene the message of Jesus' body being absent from the tomb (20:2). Both he and Peter rush to the tomb where they see the burial cloth and facial napkin that had covered Jesus. The Gospel writer says the Beloved Disciple "saw and believed" (20:8), most likely implying he believed that Jesus had overcome death despite not fully comprehending this event, while Peter is less aware and slower to understand. Once again, the Gospel writer is emphasizing the very special mutuality and closeness the Beloved Disciple enjoys with Christ. It is something the other apostles and disciples do not manifest.

Finally, the Gospel writer relates how it is the Beloved Disciple, not Peter or the others, who recognizes the risen Jesus on the lake shore when the apostles are fishing some distance away (21:1–14). Jesus is soon to host them with a breakfast of fish and bread, which alludes to the Eucharist. It is his voice and presence that the Beloved Disciple recognizes before anyone else. After the meal Peter inquires about the future of this disciple. Jesus says, "If it is my will that he remain until I come, what is that to you?" (21:22). In Jesus' response to Peter, again emphasizing the unique relationship Jesus and this disciple have, the Gospel writer adds that he is "the disciple whom Jesus loved, who had lain close to his breast at the supper" and asked the question about the identity of Jesus' betrayer (21:20). St. John's Gospel could hardly be more explicit about the unique relationship of this disciple with Jesus.

BLESSINGS FLOWING FROM THIS RELATIONSHIP

Most biblical exegetes of St. John's Gospel agree that the writer intended this theme of the Beloved Disciple to inspire imitation by those who hear this Gospel and come to faith in Jesus. The blessings and joys that flow from becoming another Beloved Disciple of Jesus are so abundant. Some of them are described by Teresa of Avila in the latter dwelling places of *The Interior Castle*.

Above all is Jesus' gift of himself to us, revealing himself as divine as well as fully human, and leading us to Abba Father as our own Abba. Jesus is totally given to his Father, and he wants us to know and love Abba as our Abba (17:3). We do not really know Jesus unless we appreciate how deeply he loves his Father. His public ministry was focused especially on revealing the Father. This is stressed in John's Gospel. There is nothing, *nothing* more beautiful and satisfying to the soul than our enjoying a loving union with Abba Father and Christ Jesus, the Source of everything! Being welcomed into this union is, indeed, to discover the pearl of great price or find the treasure buried in the field (Matt 13:44–46).

Jesus is completely given to Abba, and to us as well. As Beloved Disciples, we experience this total outpouring of Jesus to us, especially when we receive his body and blood. The sweetness of this encounter is often indescribable. One senses the depths of Jesus' love implied in the words "body" and "blood." In Jesus' culture "body" means "my whole self" and "blood" means "life." This gesture of giving his life and total self to us, which is not just a symbol or memorial, but truly Jesus, evokes sooner or later the reciprocal desire to give to him our total self. In this holy exchange, we find all we are looking for: mercy, healing, communion, meaning, love, and fulfillment. We know in our depths that the fullness of these core needs, on God's great day, will be given to us completely. We will have become another Christ,[5] realizing our deepest desires.

The poem that follows illustrates this profound bond of love between the Divine Master and one of his Beloved Disciples.

Remember

"I want the Heart of Jesus."
So simple, direct, so true.
I surprise myself by what I say
as solitude begins.

You smile, Lord,
for from all eternity
the threads of your desire have been
weaving through the years,
those lures of love gently drawing me
to yourself, growing deep within.
Now the thrusts of love explode in freedom!
The fullness of time has come.

5. For a deeper appreciation of our "Becoming another Christ," read chs. 6–9 of Owens, *More than You Could Ever Imagine.*

With outstretched hands, I offer my heart
    to you, my Lord.
And, suddenly, your Sacred Heart is
    Love's exchange.
In eternity, my heart pulses within you
    to our delight.
Here, each rhythm of my heart sings
    an eternal song:
"Behold this Heart which has
    loved you so much."

And you, Triune Love, look at me and see yourself.
    Swooping down to earth,
    you snatch up and draw into your oneness
    this beloved
    who now cradles the Heart of God.

Past, present, future are
    caught up in one Eternal Now.
And there is love, only love.[6]

The joy of the Beloved Disciple's life, then, centers around Jesus and telling others about him, pointing others to him, and taking them to meet him. This is the role of the friend of the bridegroom, seen early in John's gospel, and is the fulfillment of the search for the meaning of one's life: to evangelize, to be a matchmaker, bringing people, potential brides, to Jesus, who is the bridegroom (3:29). The Beloved Disciple, like John the Baptist, might say after seeing these divine/human marriages begin: "It is time for me to go. I did what I was called to do, what any close friend would do, and could not have done anything else that would have given me greater purpose and joy. 'He must increase, [and] I must decrease' (3:30)."

The climax of this vocation is yet to come, however. The Beloved Disciple, toward the end of the Gospel, has us observe in detail the final moments of Jesus' death, with his side being pierced with a soldier's lance and his Heart being opened with infinite, divine love. He has us note so movingly how blood and water flow from Jesus' side (19:34), alluding to the life of the church beginning there with baptism (water) and being nurtured especially through the Eucharist (blood).

After Jesus' resurrection the writer depicts the apostle St. Thomas moving from stubborn doubt to striking faith in the risen Jesus when he

6. Patricia Brewster (d. 2015), mother of seven, authored these lines while making the 30-days *Spiritual Exercises of St. Ignatius of Loyola*.

looks at the pierced hands of Jesus and places his hand in the open side of Jesus, exclaiming, "My Lord and my God!" (20:24–28). Those wanting to imitate the Beloved Disciple, as well as St. Thomas, will do the same when ministering to the wounded: placing their hand in their wounds by listening compassionately to, and praying with, them for healing. St. John finishes his testimony by saying why as a disciple he witnesses to these events: so that "you may believe that Jesus is the Christ, the Son of God, and that believing you may have life in his name" (20:31). Anyone aspiring to be a Beloved Disciple of Jesus will do in his or her own way and setting the same that this original Beloved Disciple did.

ADDITIONAL BLESSINGS

As we gain the spirit and heart of the Beloved Disciple, we will love what Jesus loves and receive with awe and gratitude any blessings he gives. In the final minutes of his life, Jesus gives his mother to the Beloved Disciple to be the Disciple's own mother (19:25–27). Like him, we will "take her unto our own" (19:27).[7] We will allow her, as the best of mothers, to intercede and care for us as we seek to belong totally to her Son and be poured out in loving service of his Gospel. Mary models for us the singleness of heart and fullness of divine life we are ultimately destined for in and through her Son. In the New Testament, she is Jesus' first disciple and powerfully instrumental in his salvific work. In the words of St. Paul, the risen Jesus is the first-born in the new creation, implying that the heavenly assumed Mary is the second-born.[8]

STILL FURTHER BLESSINGS

The Gospels of Sts. Matthew and Luke, in their treatment of the Beatitudes, depict many of the qualities and blessings found in beloved discipleship.

---

7. Bible translations from the time of the King James Version have translated this phrase to say that the beloved disciple took Mother Mary "into his home. " The Greek text of this verse does not include the word "home" but says that the Beloved Disciple took her "to his own." It could imply one's home, but more likely St. John means a deeper sense of taking her "into his care," or "into his heart," which for me is more likely intended, given the solemnity of this final moment of Jesus' life and the spiritual significance for the church's relationship to the Mother of God and hers to us.

8. Owens, "Deification," 241–63.

Taken together, the Beatitudes are a portrait of Jesus and of his closest followers, providing a vivid picture of transformation in Christ. We see there a person of great virtues, especially in the foundational ones of faith, hope, and love, which are further developed by the seven gifts (knowledge, understanding, counsel/discernment, fortitude, piety, and fear of the Lord, with wisdom being the integration of these six) and nine fruits of the Holy Spirit (love, joy, peace, patience, kindness, goodness, fidelity, gentleness and self-control). Like an inner compass or GPS, the Holy Spirit of the risen Jesus, through the gift of discernment, guides a Beloved Disciple close to Jesus so they will make wise, lifegiving choices.[9] He or she finds as well in the saints of God models and great inspiration for the kind of love and grateful service that Jesus and Abba Father deserve.

Another wonderful blessing is that of enjoying great spiritual friendships with others aspiring to become a Beloved Disciple. Aelred of Rievaulx (d. 1167), a Cistercian monk and abbot, describes in his classic work, *Spiritual Friendship*, great spiritual joy shared by those close to Jesus. Rievaulx says the distinctive trait of loving friends is their prioritizing God above all in their relationship.[10] One of their deepest satisfactions is seeing their friend come closer to God. Their distress would be to realize that they had come between God and their friend and made their friend less than what he or she could be in and with God. Spiritual friends, then, regardless of gender, complete each other's soul, discover each other's depths as well as some of the depths of God, and grow in trusting and surrendering to a love that hints at God's perfectly fulfilling joy.

Jesus the Christ, in such precious friendships, opens us to more of the mystery of our true self as well as a greater sense of the profound unity we

---

9. Joseph Cardinal Mercier (d. 1926), a Belgian spiritual directee of the renowned Blessed Dom Columba Marmion, offers this touching comment on the place of the Holy Spirit in the life of those seeking to live a holy life:

> I am going to reveal to you the secret of sanctity and happiness. Every day . . . enter into yourself . . . speak to that Divine Spirit, saying . . . 'O Holy Spirit, Soul of my soul, I adore Thee! Enlighten me, guide me, strengthen me, console me. Tell me what I should do; give me Thy orders. I promise to submit myself to all that Thou desirest of me and to accept all that Thou permittest to happen to me. Just make me know Thy Will.' If you do this, your life will flow along happily, serenely, and full of consolation, even in the midst of trials. Grace will be proportioned to the trial, giving you strength to carry it, and you will arrive at the Gate of Paradise laden with merit. This submission to the Holy Spirit is the secret of sanctity. (A Benedictine Monk, *In Sinu Jesu*, 107)

10. Aelred of Rievaulx, *Spiritual Friendship*, especially Bk. III, 91, 101, 127, 133, and 134.

are meant to realize with Abba Father and the people of God. As Jesus went to the depths of his Heart to experience in his earthly life who he is, so, too, each of us must go into the depths of our own hearts to become who we are destined to be. True spiritually grounded friendships serve this search.[11]

Last, another blessing of being a Beloved Disciple is a new strength and courage to bear with our own sufferings and to find in them an opportunity to unite our self with Jesus crucified and with our struggling neighbors who make up his mystical body (Col 1:24). A Beloved Disciple has a great capacity for showing compassion for others, to bring care to the broken-hearted and act on behalf of those who suffer injustice. At the same time a Beloved Disciple trusts God's inscrutable wisdom, is surrendered to God's providence, and is optimistic about the eventual victory of God's love over all evil and failure. He or she can maintain inside a certain peace about the future and celebrate moments when the victory of God's love shines through.

TO THE DEPTHS AND BACK

> At the heart of a contemplative there is a point of solitude where, beyond the heavens and the innermost depths of all beings, the whole universe is present for the purpose of a boundless exchange. Those who, like certain great contemplatives, seem to flee from human contacts are, in reality, moving toward this ultimate point of their being that opens out onto the infinity of God and the indeterminate stretches of [human] history.[12]

Such people go to the depths of God[13] and are energized to return to their active lives to accomplish great deeds, doing their part as co-creators in God's building the kingdom and loving the world as only a Beloved Disciple

---

11. This is beautifully expressed in the words of the French Canadian Blessed Marie Rose Durocher (d. 1849), foundress of the Sisters of the Holy Names of Jesus and Mary: "I invite you to go there [into the Heart of Jesus] with me, for it is there that I wish to remain, and where, if you wish it so, we shall never be separated from one another" (Durocher, *Pilgrimage of the Heart*, 99).

12. Raguin, *Depth of God*, 30–31.

13. One of the more apt metaphors for such an encounter is the expanse of the star-studded night sky that God showed Abraham, and which we have all gazed at in great wonder. Astronomers tell us there is no known edge to our ever-expanding cosmos, suggesting that for all eternity those in Christ will engage in a never-ending exploration of God's being, goodness, and beauty, while sharing richly in God's ecstatic joy in sharing his love for us.

can. Outstanding examples of such people are: Francis of Assisi, Gertrude of Helfta, Ignatius of Loyola, John of the Cross, Teresa of Avila, and Dominic and Catherine of Siena. Also, Mother Teresa of Kolkata, Dorothy Day, Henri Nouwen, Oscar Romero, Teilhard de Chardin, Chiara Lubich, and Catherine de Hoek Doherty.

In the depths of Jesus risen, then, we find the source and foundation of everything (i.e., the boundless, bottomless depths of God's own merciful, welcoming Heart, the ultimate Source of all reality). This Source of love, from which everyone and everything has come, is not to be confused with our own depths, as some Buddhists would say; instead, this One is wholly other with a life infinitely beyond the limits of our own person and of all creation. And yet "in the act of love God's depths become mine. I have, in fact, stepped outside the limitations of my own being to enter God's domain. I am in him and he is in me."[14] We are encouraged by God's Spirit "to follow God to the end of everything beyond all depth . . . to go by way of Christ's humanity . . . to the depths . . . as far as the Word was in God, God before all time."[15] Resting on the Heart of Christ, then, bringing ourselves there and the entire world, especially the crucified of today's world,[16] opens us to this Mystery of merciful, patient love. This Gracious Mystery attracts our soul to stay faithful to the journey as Teresa of Avila describes in her castle/soul with its seven dwelling places. All along that way we experience God ever new, at each stage like never before.[17]

14. Raguin, *Depth of God*, 71.

15. Raguin, *Depth of God*, 88–89.

16. Pope Francis often emphasizes how it is in the poor we find a privileged place to encounter Christ, that we meet him quite readily in those who are the marginalized and vulnerable, in the victims of war, human trafficking, xenophobia, drugs, and the selfish pursuit of national interests. In them we have a mirror of our own poverty and can get in touch with our own need for salvation. We go, then, to the poor and the crucified to meet Jesus and to be saved.

17. St. Bernard of Clairvaux (d. 1153) says:

> I think that even when it has found him the soul will not cease to seek him. God is sought not on foot but by desire. And the happy discovery of what is desired does not end desire but extends it. The consummation of joy does not consume desire, does it? Rather, it is oil poured on flames, which itself catches fire. Thus it is. Joy will be fulfilled . . . But there will be no end to desire, and so no end of seeking. (Bernard of Clairvaux, "Sermon 84," 274).

A CLOSING AFTERTHOUGHT: A SPECIAL
WAY INTO CHRIST'S HEART

We recall from John's Gospel (19:34; 20:28) how the risen Jesus showed his five wounds to his disciples. This scriptural detail has attracted throughout Christian history countless people to the wounds of the crucified, risen Christ,[18] Thomas the Apostle and St. Francis of Assisi being the best-known examples.

We have the same opportunity in our prayer to ask for and carry within our spirit what St. Gertrude of Helfta (d. 1302) called an *interior* stigmata (i.e., "the marks of [Jesus'] love impressed on my heart."[19]). The interior stigmata may be experienced as the shared grief and compassion of carrying within ourselves the wounded members of the body of Christ, or in our experiencing a deep sadness in so many people not knowing God or being too busy to seek him (Luke 19:41–44). It can also come from our being pierced by a deep betrayal or our own failure; by a false accusation and subsequent damaged reputation; or by the loss of a great friend and/or love in our life. We, too, can aspire to this intimacy and depth. St. Gertrude petitioned this extraordinary favor through a prayer in her book, *Herald of Divine Love*. Stated below, it is an abbreviation and contemporary paraphrase of the prayer she found. It expresses what seems quite characteristic of the spirit of the Beloved Disciple:

> Inscribe with your precious blood, most merciful Lord, your five sacred wounds in my depths so that I may read and ponder therein how much you suffered and how deeply you love us. May the memory of these wounds ever remain in the deepest parts of my soul to stir within me your compassionate sorrow and inflame my heart with divine love.[20]

With St. Francis of Assisi's inspiration we can add:

18. Devotion to the wounds of Christ greatly flourished in the early and middle medieval times of Germany and nations near it. Also, it is part of a long-standing tradition in the liturgies of Eastern Christianity to include crosses with jewels mounted in the places of the five wounds of Jesus.

19. Gertrude, *Herald of Divine Love*, 101.

20. Gertrude, *Herald of Divine Love*, 100.

May the power of your love, Lord, fiery and sweet as honey, wean my heart from all that is under heaven, so that I may die for love of your love, you who were so good as to die for love of my love.[21]

Teresa of Avila knew God so well and wrote *The Interior Castle* to lead others to the One who is the Gracious Mystery of unbounded love. Let us now move to the last chapter and take a close look at the God Jesus reveals to us as boundless truth, mercy, and love through the eyes of St. Teresa.

QUESTIONS FOR DISCUSSION AND FAITH-SHARING

- How would you explain the phrase, "he took her unto his own," in reference to Mother Mary, a gift from Jesus, in his final moments of life, given to the Beloved Disciple? What are some of the implications of that gift? What are some of the church's spiritual riches reflected in that phrase?

- In what way have you been blessed with friends in a relationship you would call a spiritual friendship? Read footnotes 10 and 11 before answering this question.

- Why would it be said that we do not really know Jesus until we know/ experience something of his Abba Father as our Abba? (Using the name Amma for God is perfectly consistent with Jesus' wanting us to enjoy for ourselves much of the closeness he experiences with God.) Explain.

- Have you had any experience of meeting Jesus in the poor and wounded, seeing and listening to the broken-hearted and those who are crucified by life? Tell your story if you have one, please. See footnote 16 above. Can you say you have experienced something of your own poverty mirrored back to you by meeting them?

---

21. See Canettieri, *Amor de Caritate*, Canticle III, Stanzas 28, 31–33.

14

How Teresa Sees God

WHAT IS GOD LIKE? What divine attributes get emphasized in Teresa of Avila's *The Interior Castle* when she explains how God brings forth our deepest desires and divine potential?

GOD AS TRUTH

What emerges above all is that God is Truth, the One who relates to us only as Truth and in truth, and who will not accept anything less, even if it takes us a long time to come to such self-transparency. Besides being Truth itself, God is also infinite patience and mercy; he works with us until we trust him enough and finally let go of everything we were blind to, holding on to, or denying. In the end, however, thanks to his very nature and for our own greater good, God cannot be anything but Truth. This becomes increasingly apparent in the later dwelling places when God's Spirit will respectfully press us more and more for the fullness of our truth. He purges us radically during the later stages of our journey, refining us to live from our deepest desires. As St. John says in 1 John 1:5, "God is Light, and in him is no darkness at all."

Being Truth himself, the essence of humble purity and enticing beauty, God becomes more compelling when we recall the many times Teresa insists on humility and truthfulness with ourselves if we are going to grow in God's life. If God is so humble and good, so giving and truthful, how can we be anything else if we hope to share in a great friendship and deep, mutual love? Recall Teresa's startling and sad statement that many in the third dwelling places choose to settle there for the rest of their lives; that their choice comes from fearing to know themselves in their weaknesses and from not knowing and trusting God enough. In many respects they make themselves the center of their lives rather than God. Very likely they assume, and wrongly so, that the revelation of certain humbling truths about themselves in God's presence, something he ironically already knows, will make them less lovable and welcomed by him. God is not yet important enough for them to risk everything and launch out into a new way of living with and for Jesus.

One implication of this emphasis on God as Truth is a growing sensitivity to and dis-ease with the world's love for money, its greed and lust for power, and its often-scandalous compromising of truth in the circles of economics, politics, government, and church, in addition to its use of deception and violence to cloak and defend its interests. This awareness of societal sin, a major component of a mature Christian faith life, will manifest itself in care for the poor, the marginalized, the dispossessed, and the orphans and widows of the world—namely, the victims of those living out of greed and violence. They will speak out for justice, even if doing so incurs disapproval, being judged as sexist or unpatriotic, or even risking not receiving a promotion in the secular or ecclesial world. These sensitivities of God's Holy Spirit will make us increasingly take on God's Heart and be more inclusive, even global, in our prayers of petition and service.

I wish to emphasize God's manner when leading us to these deeper sensitivities toward the poor and dispossessed: it is by way of invitation. He is always respectful toward us, just as Jesus was so respectful toward the rich young man. God never violates the freedom he gives us, never forces on us knowledge about our self. He walks with us, step by step, until we are ready to receive more of our truth and that of the world around us, until we want to invite him more deeply into our life. How extraordinary is his way of loving us! This point leads us to the next trait of God implied in Teresa's writing.

GOD AS GOODNESS AND UNENDING MERCY

While God's truth and purity will mirror back and expose any lack of integrity and wholeness in us, it is his ever-giving goodness and kindness, his tender mercies, his constant welcome that usually attract us to him most. Such is true even when having to face our sinfulness, our self-centered ways, and a deepening appreciation of our need for a Savior. It is knowing and coming to love deeply the Jesus of the Gospels, gained through daily contemplative prayer, that makes this saving truth come alive for us and enables us to trust and want to return love. Divine goodness and mercy, then, are, together, the second of the outstanding traits of God in Teresa's book.

When addressing this theme of God's lovableness, Teresa is speaking from her personal experience and the profound wisdom she was given in the very demanding challenges she faced during the last twenty-seven years of her life. Beginning at age forty, after twenty years in religious life, she was given the grace to live her vocation without any compromise, to live for God with all her heart, soul, mind, and strength, and pour herself out into the reform of her Carmelite sisters. With such a life-changing gift from God, she showed a profound trust of, and obedience to, God despite many clerics who ill-served her, suspecting her of the worst, calling her a fraud, spiritually deluded, and dangerous. As a result, she almost stopped her efforts to reform Carmel. These terrible sufferings served as God's providential ways of purifying her heart of anything not of God and blessing her with a singular wisdom that has proven so helpful to countless others.

At the heart of her wisdom is Teresa's lifelong experience and firm conviction that God comes to us above all in Jesus. Jesus is the embodiment of divine love and comes to us in our human reality. Experiencing him relating to us so personally in our daily life is what makes the Good News so convincing and freeing. To encounter him as the embodiment of loving mercy and unconditional acceptance is powerfully compelling, even life-changing. Teresa experienced Jesus this way so many times; it enabled her to be faithful, especially during the purifying experiences of the sixth dwelling places. There is never a time in any of Teresa's dwelling places when we move beyond Jesus and his humanity. The love of God comes into the human condition and always works in and with us as we are, never in some disembodied spiritual state, no matter how advanced we may be in God's Spirit. Our destiny is to be transformed in Christ, the God-*Man*; it is to become another Christ, not someone who is only spirit.

Toward the close of *The Interior Castle*, Teresa counsels her sisters, and implicitly anyone who wants to know deeply and needs to cling to God, to "fix your eyes on the Crucified [One] and all will be small for you."[1] She

1. *IC*, VII, 4, 8.

urges us, in effect, to gaze lovingly into the eyes of Jesus, to be steadily present to his pierced and open heart, to let Abba Father invite us to enter and bring there our pains and those of the world.

Teresa was not formally educated in theology. Such was not an option for women in sixteenth-century Spain. But it is quite evident that God taught her very well in prayer and blessed her not only with amazing wisdom but also with a remarkable sense of humor, of common sense, and of the common good. She was amazingly balanced, practical, intelligent, and blessed with great determination of will and impressive intuitive and imaginative powers. All these gifts helped her realize her mission of leading the reform of her sisters. She lived completely open to whatever was of God: the true, the good, and the beautiful. She was too good a friend of his to relate with any other kind of attitude.

GOD AS TRINITARIAN MYSTERY

What Teresa knew well and was so enlightened by throughout *The Interior Castle* is what Jesus talks about when the seventy disciples he had sent out on their first mission return. They are jubilant over what happens when they act in his name and are instrumental in miraculous healings, exorcisms, and transformations of people with faith (Luke 10:17–24). Jesus rejoices with them over their experiences of the coming of the kingdom and "seeing Satan fall from heaven." He then calls their attention to what is cause for even greater jubilation when he says their names are written in heaven, implicitly in the heart of Abba Father (10:20). He does this by sharing what is deepest in his own soul. For Jesus it is the most profound of all revelations in his teachings.

St. Luke describes Jesus as not just rejoicing in this scene but *exulting in the Holy Spirit*—exulting, so overflowing with joy is he. Why? Because the Father has revealed to them more fully than ever who Jesus is: namely, the Son and beloved of the Father; also, because, thanks to Jesus revealing the true heart of God, they now know God in a very beautiful, tender way as Abba Father (10:22). Jesus stresses how many prophets and ancient kings longed to see and hear what they were experiencing but never did (10:23–24). So, too, was Teresa blessed to see with the eyes of her heart Abba Father and Jesus in all their tenderness, gentleness, wisdom, purity of spirit, humble love, and majesty.

There are gifts of God that are so beautiful and meaningful, tailored to what each of us needs in our spiritual journey. The greatest of all gifts God gives, however, is his own self, along with an intimate awareness of, and appreciation for, how deep and personal is his love for us. This is the gift for which Jesus was congratulating his disciples.

When we awaken to God's personal love for us and rest in him, an ocean of love, we discover that his depths have no limits, no boundaries, no bottom or ceiling. It is in the embrace of the Father and the Son that we live. All of creation is destined to live, move, and have the fullness of our being, forever, in this unlimited love (Acts 17:28). Till then, all creation is converging on the Heart of the risen Christ. We are on our way home to an eternal communion of universal friendship (Isa 55:10–11; 1 Cor 15:28). Our love, divinized and maximized by the gifts of the Holy Spirit, will beautifully image our divine origin: the infinite, eternal love of the Father for the Son and of the Son for the Father.[2] It is their love for each other, who is the Holy Spirit, that acts like a magnet evoking our own deepest desires.

Might we imagine Jesus, with tears in his eyes, being almost breathless when speaking about this in Luke 10:21–24? When congratulating his disciples, the Holy Spirit was welling up through his whole being. He was sharing how Abba Father is the greatest joy of his life. He desires the same for us, through knowing and loving him, in a life of pouring ourselves out, as he has done for us.

GOD THE INDEFATIGABLE WORKER

It is striking how Teresa, when describing the fifth and especially the seventh dwelling places, emphasizes quite strongly the necessity of good works as a sign confirming our being in the later dwelling places of the castle, and that these works must be done with great love. It is true that Teresa does not speak of God as one who is doing good works, but it seems fair enough to see God imaged this way in her writings when, as she stresses, the person is doing good works toward their neighbor out of great love for, and the desire to imitate, Christ. Remember that Second Isaiah (Isa 40–55) speaks of God still creating and of our being called to be co-creators with God. Remember also in John's Gospel Jesus describing how he and the Father are "at work" even now (5:17). Biblical passages like these, then, provide a good basis for imaging God as One who is at work.

2. See Owens, *More than You Could Ever Imagine*, ch. 8.

Teresa was a cloistered religious woman and wrote *The Interior Castle* for her fellow sisters, not so much for those in a more active way of life. She would never have been permitted by church authorities in those inquisitional times to distribute her book to the public. It makes sense, then, that her vision of God with respect to work and his ongoing creation was confined largely to the reforms she had initiated for her Carmelite sisters. It seems proper, then, to draw out some implications about God in Teresa's great emphasis on good works as an essential expression of the spirituality of anyone blessed to live in the later dwelling places. To do this I draw upon certain key insights in the Ignatian tradition, from the Jesuit religious order begun in 1540 by St. Ignatius of Loyola (d. 1556), a contemporary of Teresa. Hopefully, this will contribute to helping those who live the active life in the world (e.g., raising families and staffing schools, hospitals, factories, farms, financial services, etc.) to apply Teresa's teachings to their own situations.

IGNATIUS SHARES MUCH WITH TERESA

It is in the building of the kingdom, which is a unique way for God and God's people to live and work together in peace and compassion, in loving service of others, that Ignatius saw God working in history and for all times. He describes God in the "Contemplatio," the final prayer exercise of his *Spiritual Exercises,* as one who "labors" with what some have likened to the intensity of a pregnant woman struggling, sometimes with much pain, to birth her child. Ignatius felt so strongly, like Teresa, the pain and cost of God's laboring expressed especially in the passion and death of Jesus. He envisioned God struggling in, through, and even beyond the church to the very ends of the world, while engaged in *one great work* to save and transform the entire human family. This was the work, the mission God gave Jesus. This will be our mission and work as well if we are willing to accept this awesome call as the meaning of our life. There we will readily find God.

There is, then, a deep resonance between Teresa's emphasis on good works and Ignatius's vision of God humbly birthing us in Christ. At the same time, Ignatius, both in the kingdom meditation of his *Spiritual Exercises* and *The Constitutions of the Society of Jesus* which he authored, sees God summoning men and women to *cooperate with him* in his laboring to bring forth this new world[3], what St. Paul calls a *pleroma* or fullness in Christ (Col 2:9–10). Such people, as disciples of Jesus, will be imitating the God who

---

3. Ignaius of Loyola, *Constitutions of the Society of Jesus,* sec. 138.

is engaged in good works, glorifying him in so doing, radiating something of the refulgence of divine goodness, truth, and beauty. Like Teresa in her emphasis on humility and self-knowledge, Ignatius stresses that to live such an exalted call, we must engage in certain disciplines of body and soul, especially of our will with its tendencies toward self-centered choices.

I close this book by pointing to the event in the life of Jesus when he expresses the best and most meaningful of God's works, the event that moves and motivates us, probably more than any other event in his life, to cooperate with him and Abba Father in their saving and transforming the world. It is the story that so often moves men and women to live no longer for themselves but for Jesus and to permit God's Spirit to lead them into the deeper parts of their interior castle. I refer to the passion of Jesus, but specifically to its being lived now in the body of Christ, the people of our day. I see Jesus crucified, where Teresa counsels us to fix our eyes, in the following story. I was blessed to hear it from an eyewitness when guiding her as a retreatant. I acknowledge the story will be distressing for some, not unlike how the crucifixion of Jesus was terribly distressing for those who were there that day. I offer it as an example of the triumph in Christ of the human spirit over oppression, over the will to impose and control. It demonstrates the power of the resurrection that God offers us in Christ to heal from all our sufferings and to live with an indomitable hope that God's love has the last say.

JESUS, JOY OF MAN'S DESIRING: A STORY

In a village of Sudan there was a young married couple with child. Desperate for work, the husband moved hundreds of miles north to Khartoum, the capital city. The wife found work as a cook for a community of Catholic missionary priests ministering in a parish. She had grown up in a pagan family. Her mother was a witch doctor in her village and performed witchcraft rituals according to the people's needs. The desire for vengeance was not uncommon among the people of the village and some would seek out her mother to call out evil spirits against their enemies.

While preparing meals for the missionaries, the young woman would overhear in the next room a teacher catechizing the Christian children. Her son, seven years old, wanted to be with the other children, so she let him join them. Rarely had she heard anything about Jesus, but this time she was drawn to learn more about him and his passion and how he suffered it out

167

of love and for the salvation of everyone, "even" as she was told, "for Afri-cans." Bits and pieces of this story stayed with her and became the focus of her thoughts while preparing meals. In stark contrast to what she had heard and witnessed in her mother's rituals, she learned that Jesus taught: "Love your enemies, pray for those who persecute you" and "if someone slaps you on one cheek, turn to them the other" (Matt 5:44, 5:39).

During her husband's three-year absence, she became a Christian, even a catechist, while he had become a Muslim. He now had a second wife and young daughter and had returned to bring her and their boy with him to his new home and place of work. Expecting her to come with him, the husband was infuriated to hear her say no, that she was choosing to stay behind with their son rather than go with him as one of his wives. The vil-lage elders told her she and their boy had to go with her husband. She again said no and was threatened with a public flogging. Persistently, in the face of this threat, she steadfastly said no.

On the next Saturday, most in the camp gathered, tense with emotions, to witness her punishment. She was publicly threatened again but remained determined. The judge reminded her that her disobedience would cost her 138 lashes. She responded, "Go ahead. I prefer to die as a Christian." While standing at a pole with her wrists tied to it and her dress still covering her back, two elders, standing on either side of her, alternated strokes. Many of the women, gathered in the large circle of onlookers and often peeking out from behind their head-cover, shrieked, wailed, and wept. They knew what it was like as a woman to be treated this way. The woman herself cried out at times but never cursed or said anything hateful nor threatened revenge.

There was a deathly silence when the whipping concluded. Everyone waited to see whether she was still alive after such a vicious beating. She was untied, given water, and allowed time to regain normal breathing. The women soon came forward to her aid, took her to a nearby hut and, after washing her, applied herbs to her back and some oils to help her heal. She convalesced for over two months while having to sleep face down. With the care and love of these good women, she healed quite well.

Someone asked this amazing woman what possessed her to submit to and endure such a beating. She said that when overhearing what her boy was learning with the Christian children, she was very taken by the story of Jesus being publicly flogged, that he died for everyone, even, as she said, "for me and for everyone." She was so struck that he did this out of love, and especially that he did not curse or say hateful words but, above all, forgave those who had conspired to execute him. She said she felt strength from him, even close to him during her sorriest moment, and that this gave her the desire and hope to survive her horrible ordeal. She wanted to come to know Jesus much more and desired the same for her boy.

IN CONCLUSION

When we truly meet Jesus, and through him, Abba Father, we will experience something of what this amazing, heroic woman experienced. As he did for St. Teresa and this woman, the risen Jesus will draw out of our depths the best and most beautiful parts of ourselves, our deepest desires. We will know the overwhelming love of God and be moved to give all we have and are in return, from our substance, like the poor widow did in Luke 21:1–4 with her two coins.

When we cross over into God, our substance or two coins will be infinitely expanded, transformed in Christ. Jesus has promised this! Images of God, we will realize the fullness of our baptism and be able to relate to God and all creation, human and otherwise, with total mutuality (Rom 8:21–23). Made divine or another Christ, each of us, stunningly transfigured, will radiate this Triune God living in our depths and in the communion of saints. The plan of God to save and gather all his children into one family will have been realized (1 Cor 15:28). We who trusted in Jesus the Christ, or simply *tried* to trust in him, will have finally come home to God, whose joy it is to welcome and love us forever.

Praise be Jesus Christ, the joy of man's and woman's desiring, now and forever. May Mary, his mother, to whom this book is dedicated, be loved and honored forever as our dear mother. Finally, we must exclaim: Glory to the Father, and to the Son, and to the Holy Spirit—as it was in the beginning, is now, and will be forever. Amen!

QUESTIONS FOR DISCUSSION AND FAITH-SHARING

- What is most significant for you in the closing story? What spiritual message and challenge does it carry for you? How does it compare with the story of Peter van der Broek in chapter 12?

- In the meditation that concludes the Spiritual Exercises of St. Ignatius, it is said God "labors" in the passion of Jesus, like a woman laboring to give birth to a child. What does this image of God say to you about what God is doing in history, in your own life, and in the lives of others? What does it say about what the world means to God? And about what you mean to God?

Bibliography

Aelred of Rievaulx. *Spiritual Friendship.* Kalamazoo, MI: Cistercian, 1977.

Assagioli, Roberto. *Act of Will: A Guide to Self-Actualization & Self-Realization.* Florence, Italy: The Synthesis Center, 1973.

—. *Psychosynthesis: A Manual of Principles and Techniques.* New York: HarperCollins, 1993.

—. *Transpersonal Development.* Toronto: Penguin, 2008.

Benedictine Monk, A. *In Sinu Jesu: When Heart Speaks to Heart: The Journal of a Priest at Prayer.* Kettering, OH: Angelico, 2016.

Bergoglio, Jorge Cardinal (Pope Francis). *The Way of Humility: Corruption and Sin, On Self-Accusation.* San Francisco: Ignatius, 2014.

Bernard of Clairvaux. "Sermon 84." In *Selected Works of St. Bernard of Clairvaux: The Classics of Western Spirituality,* edited by John Farina, 274–78. New York: Paulist, 1987.

Boase, Leonard. *The Prayer of Faith.* Chicago: Loyola University Press, 1985.

Bonaventure, Saint. *Bonaventure: The Soul's Journey into God, The Tree of Life, The Life of St. Francis.* Translated by Ewert Cousins. New York: Paulist, 1978.

Brewster, Patricia. "Remember," unpublished poem.

Brockman, James. *Romero: A Life.* Maryknoll, NY: Orbis, 1989.

Burrows, Ruth. *Fire upon the Earth, The "Interior Castle" Explored: St. Teresa's Teachings on the Life of Deep Union.* Denville, NJ: Dimension, 1981.

Canettieri, Paolo. *Canticle III; Amor de Caritate.* McAdenville, NC: Sensus Fidelium, 2002.

Ciszek, Walter J., with Dan Flaherty. *He Leadeth Me: An Extraordinary Testimony of Faith.* Garden City, NY: Doubleday, 1975.

Conner, James L., and Fellows of the Woodstock Theological Center. *The Dynamism of Desire: Bernard J.F. Lonergan, SJ, on "The Spiritual Exercises of Saint Ignatius of Loyola."* St. Louis: Institute of Jesuit Studies, 2006.

Coombs, Marie Theresa, and Francis Kelly Nemeck. *O Blessed Night: Recovering from Addiction, Codependency and Attachment, Based on the Insights of St. John of the Cross and Pierre Teilhard de Chardin.* New York: Alba, 1991.

—. *The Way of Spiritual Direction.* Collegeville, MN: Liturgical, 1985.

Delio, Ilia. *Crucified Love: Bonaventure's Mysticism of the Crucified Christ.* Quincy, IL: Franciscan, 1998.

Downey, Michael. *Altogether Gift: A Trinitarian Spirituality.* Maryknoll, NY: Orbis, 2000.

Durocher, Marie Rose. *Pilgrimage of the Heart with Mother Marie Rose to the Sacred Sites.* Longueuil, QC: SNJM Charism Office, 2010.

Fleming, David L. *Draw Me into Your Friendship: The Spiritual Exercises: A Literal Translation of Ignatius' Spiritual Exercises & a Contemporary Reading.* St. Louis: Institute of Jesuit Sources, 1996.

Francis, Pope. *Joy of the Gospel.* Nairobi: Paulines, Africa, 2014.

Gabriel of St. Mary Magdalene. *From the Sacred Heart to the Trinity: The Spiritual Legacy of St. Teresa Margaret (Redi) of the Sacred Heart, OCD.* Washington, DC: ICS, 2006.

Galilea, Segundo. *Following Jesus.* Maryknoll, NY: Orbis, 1985.

Gallagher, Michael Paul. *Free to Believe: Ten Steps to Faith.* Chicago: Loyola University Press, 1987.

Gertrude of Helfta. *The Herald of Divine Love.* New York: Paulist, 1991.

Glotin, Edouardo. *Sign of Salvation: The Sacred Heart of Jesus.* New Hyde Park, NY: Apostleship of Prayer, 1989.

Green, Stanley. "When We Are Reconciled, We Are Free." *The Canadian Mennonite* 4.17 (2000) 11.

Green, Thomas H. *When the Well Runs Dry: Prayer Beyond the Beginnings.* Notre Dame, IN: Ave Maria, 1979.

Halaska, Margaret. "Covenant." In *Review for Religious*, edited by David L. Fleming, 357 St. Louis: Jesuit Archives and Research Center, 1981.

Hassel, David. *Radical Prayer.* Newark, NJ: Paulist, 1983.

Hellwig, Monika K. *Understanding Catholicism.* New York, Paulist, 1981.

Ignatius of Loyola, Saint. *The Autobiography of St. Ignatius Loyola, with Related Documents.* Edited by John C. Olin. Translated by Joseph F. O'Callaghan. New York: Harper & Row, 1974.

Jalics, Franz. *Called to Share in HIS Life: Introduction to a Contemplative Way of Life and the Jesus Prayer (a Retreat).* Mumbai: St. Paul's Press, 2010.

John of the Cross, Saint. *The Ascent of Mt. Carmel.* In *The Collected Works of St. John of the Cross*, translated by Kieran Kavanaugh and Otilio Rodriguez, 68–292. Washington, DC: ICS, 1973.

———. "Counsels to a Religious on How to Reach Perfection." In *Collected Works of St. John of the Cross*, translated by Kieran Kavanagh & Otilio Rodriguez, 662–65. Washington, DC: ICS, 1973.

———. *The Dark Night.* In *The Collected Works of St. John of the Cross*, translated by Kieran Kavanaugh and Otilio Rodriguez, 295–389. Washington, DC: ICS, 1973.

———. "The Living Flame of Love." In *The Collected Works of St. John of the Cross*, translated by Kieran Kavanaugh and Otilio Rodriquez, 569–649. Washington, DC: ICS, 1973.

———. "The Precautions." In *Collected Works of St. John of the Cross*, translated by Kieran Kavanagh & Otilio Rodriguez, 656–61. Washington, DC: ICS, 1973.

Kavanaugh, Kieran. "Preface." In *Words of Wisdom for Our World: The Precautions and Counsels of St. John of the Cross*, by Susan Muto, 7–9. Eugene, OR: Wipf & Stock, 1996.

Keating, Thomas. *Open Mind, Open Heart: The Contemplative Dimension of the Gospel.* New York: Continuum, 1996.

Kinerk, E. Edward. "Eliciting Great Desires: Their Place in the Spirituality of the Society of Jesus." *St. Louis: The American Assistancy on Jesuit Spirituality* 5 (November, 1984) 1–29.

Laird, Martin. *Into the Silent Land: A Guide to the Christian Practice of Contemplation.* New York: Oxford, 2006.

Lohfink, Gerhard. *Jesus of Nazareth: What He Wanted, Who He Was.* Collegeville, MN: Liturgical, 2012.

Madeleine of St. Joseph. *Within the Castle with St. Teresa of Avila.* Translated and Abridged by the Carmel of Pittford, New York. Chicago: Franciscan Herald, 1982.

Main, John. *Word into Silence: A Manual for Christian Meditation.* Norwich, UK: Canterbury, 2014.

May, Gerald G. *Will and Spirit: A Contemplative Psychology.* San Francisco: HarperCollins, 1985.

Metz, Johannes. *Poverty of Spirit.* New York: Newman, 1968.

Miller, Frederick. *The Trial of Faith of St. Therese of Lisieux.* Staten Island, NY: Society of St. Paul, 1998.

Mother Teresa. *Mother Teresa: Come Be My Light: The Private Writings of the "Saint of Calcutta."* Edited by Brian Kolodiejchuk. New York: Doubleday, 2007.

Muto, Susan. *Where Lovers Meet: Inside the Interior Castle.* Washington, DC: Institute of Carmelite Studies, 2008.

———. *Words of Wisdom for Our World: The Precautions and Counsels of St. John of the Cross.* Eugene, OR: Wipf & Stock, 1996.

Nicolas, Adolpho. "Depth, Universality, and Learned Ministry: Challenges to Jesuit Higher Education Today; Remarks for 'Networking Jesuit Higher Education. Shaping the Future for a Humane, Just, Sustainable Globe.'" An Address given to Ignatian Educators at the Ignatian Spirituality Center in Rome, April 23, 2010.

Niere, Mary. *The Gospel of Contemplation.* Bacolod City, Philippines: Home Resources DTP, 1994.

Nouwen, Henri J. M. *The Return of the Prodigal Son: A Story of Homecoming.* New York: Doubleday, 1992.

O'Sullivan, Tracy. *Pilgrimage to God: A Pastoral Theology for Pastors and Parishioners.* Darien, IL: Carmelite Media, 2015.

Owens, Bernie. "Deification." In *With All the Fullness of God: Deification in Christian Tradition,* edited by Jared Ortiz, 241–63. Lanham, MD: Rowman & Littlefield, 2021.

———. *More than You Could Ever Imagine: On Our Becoming Divine.* Collegeville, MN: Liturgical, 2015.

Plank, Karl A. "When An 'A-Dieu' Takes on a Face: The Last Testament of Christian de Cherge', OCSO." *Spiritual Life* 53.3 (2007) 136–47.

Plato. *The Republic.* Edited by Paul Negri and Joslyn T. Pine. Mineola, NY: Dover, 2000.

Raguin, Yves. *The Depth of God.* Weathampstead Hertfordshire, UK: Clarke, 1979.

Rolheiser, Ronald. *The Shattered Lantern: Rediscovering a Felt Presence of God.* New York: Crossroads, 2004.

Rosenberg, Marshall B. *Nonviolent Communication: A Language of Life.* Encinitas, CA: PuddleDancer, 2003.

Rowe, Margaret. *God Is Love: St. Teresa Margaret, Her Life.* Washington, DC: ICS, 2003.

Seelaus, Vilma. *Distractions in Prayer: Blessing or Curse? St. Teresa of Avila's Teachings in the Interior Castle.* Canfield, OH: Society of St. Paul, 2005.

Shea, Henry J. "The Beloved Disciple and the *Spiritual Exercises*." *Studies in the Spirituality of Jesuits* 49/2 (Summer 2017) 1–35.

Sheldrake, Philip. *Befriending Our Desires.* London: Darton, Longman & Todd, 1994.

Bibliography

Sparough, J., et al. *What's Your Decision?: How to Make Choices with Confidence and Clarity: An Ignatian Approach to Decision Making.* Chicago: Loyola University Press, 2010.

Teresa of Avila. *The Interior Castle.* In *The Collected Works of St. Teresa of Avila,* vol. 2, translated by Kieran Kavanaugh and Otilio Rodriguez, 2:263–452. 3 vols. Washington, DC: ICS, 1980.

Thoreau, Henry David. *Walden.* Edited by Jeffrey S. Cramer. New Haven: Yale University Press, 2004.

Tillich, Paul. "You Are Accepted." In *The Shaking of the Foundations,* edited by Maxwell Perkins, 153–63. New York: Scribner's, 1948.

Trueblood, David Elton. *Abraham Lincoln: Theologian of American Anguish.* New York: Harper & Row, 1973.

Tugwell, Simon. *The Beatitudes: Soundings in Christian Traditions.* Springfield, IL: Templegate, 1980.

Turner, Denys. *The Darkness of God: Negativity in Christian Mysticism.* Cambridge, MA: Cambridge University Press. 1995.

Walsh, James, ed. *The Cloud of Unknowing.* Classics of Western Spirituality Series. Mahwah, NJ: Paulist, 1981.

CPSIA information can be obtained
at www.ICGtesting.com
Printed in the USA
BVHW031111090722
641621BV00006B/157

9 781666 732955